AF348697

"Annie's story, *Faith You Can Borrow,* is a story about amazing challenges, many mysteries, persevering faith, and the sufficiency of a sovereign God. She has woven her struggles into a story of grace and faith that we can share and from which we can learn again that God and our relationship with him is 'far more important and significant than any circumstance' in our lives."

Senior Pastor Larry Kirk, Christ Community Church, Daytona Beach, Florida.

"Out of the depths of her own despair and triumph, Annie Hickey has penned a story of faith and hope: faith in the God who heals and hope for those darkest hours when doctors can only shake their heads."

David Hobbs, author of *Out of the Fire*

Faith You Can Borrow
By Annie Hickey

FAITH
You Can Borrow

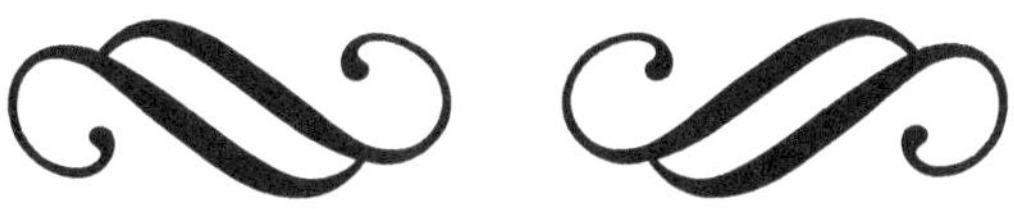

Revealing God's Faithfulness in the Face of Uncertainty

Annie Hickey

ISBN: 978-1-964462-31-8 (sc)
ISBN: 978-1-964462-32-5 (e)

Rev. date: 06/11/2024

Acknowledgements

I would like to express my appreciation to my neurologist, Dr. Alyn Benezette. Without Dr. Benezette's care and concern, I am quite certain that I would not be alive to write this book. Thank you so much for putting your patients first. Thank you for never giving up.

I would also like to express my sincere gratitude to Pastor Matt Walker. Thank you for always having time to listen and for never running out of patience. I pray that God blesses you richly for you give so much to those you shepherd.

There were so many people who reached out to help me during this stressful period of my life. Lillian Keziah has for over twenty years now been a second mother to me. My sisters were my lifeline. Blake Thomas was my constant source of encouragement. Belinda Shorts, Pam Atkinson, and Joyce Saunders gave so much of their time to sit with me in hospitals. You were truly God's angels of mercy. A special thank you to all of the body of Christ at Christ Community Church in Daytona Beach, Florida who did so much to help and never stopped praying for my recovery.

I also want to take time to acknowledge the comfort extended to me by some very special people. My friend Jeremy Brookins was so faithful to walk with me through this journey. I have very much enjoyed all of our conversations and all of your insight. My long-time friend Selina Surles never allowed those gaps in our friendship to become permanent. She stayed and doctored my hurts and cleaned my wounds and only a true friend would do that. Selina, you have the heart of a missionary. My friend Troy Schake was so faithful and firm. He never stopped believing that I would get well. He stuck by me even when others did not.

Most of my life, including the events that led to the writing of this book, would have been very different if not for the influences of my oldest and dearest friend Doug Williams. Doug, I have often said that you are my vivid reminder of heaven and God's love. I have been truly blessed by heaven itself to have such a godly man for such a friend. I stand in awe that God placed you by his divine plan in my life. I pray that our friendship lasts forever. After forty-three years, it has a pretty good start.

Dedication

This book is dedicated to God who is my strength and my ever-present help and to my children, Cassidy and Justin Elijah, who are God's most precious gifts to me and my reason for trying so hard to get well. Mommy loves you both very much!

Contents

Foreword

Sometimes I try to talk myself into having more faith and responding to life in a spiritual way, but true faith requires more than pulling myself up by my spiritual bootstraps. The "trying harder" idea of faith is not strong enough to sustain the weight of life, not during the times when life knocks me over like a cold, salty, ocean wave. I try to stand up, my mouth full of water, my shorts full of sand, and my lungs gasping for air, but I stumble under the surf because of my ever-shifting footing. Moments before, I was standing waist deep in the ocean, feet firmly planted in the shifting sand. I was simply enjoying the view. Now stumbling in the water, I wonder if will ever be able to enjoy the ocean. I don't trust the ocean and her random waves.

Perhaps the wave metaphor is too dramatic, but where is my faith in such a time? A business partner who betrays me, children making poor decisions, a late phone call from the emergency room, bad news from a doctor, stubborn sin patterns—these are the things that seem too weighty for feel good platitudes about faith. It is at times like this that we often hear well-meaning sayings such as, "This will strengthen your faith," or "This is testing your faith," or "This is when you need your faith the most." I wonder if we really believe these words. Do we really believe that faith is under human control? Is faith something we can work up? Is it like a comb in my pocket that I need to simply pull out and use? Don't misunderstand; I really want to have a strong faith, but I wonder how that faith is actually developed.

How does confident faith grow from theses moments of chaos and despair? We must be careful; God is not a formula. We do not have *steps* to deeper faith. The faith that emerges from chaos is ultimately a gift from God. Yet there are some things that seem to move us toward a gift of real faith. What must be present in the chaos for faith to grow is humility. Our tendency may be to become self-reliant or to numb ourselves with our busy strategies. However, we cry out to God. We have made this request: God will you please heal, God, will you protect my child, my spouse, my parents? *Oh Father, will you please be present?* God gives faith in the midst of chaos, not because we have taken the proper steps but because he has given grace to the humble. Much of practical Christian living begins with humility. We must acknowledge that we need God's perspective and intervention—we must enter into our questions and doubt and humbly bring them before him.

So, you cry out. We've all been there, crying out, "How long, O LORD? Will you forget me forever? How long will you hide your face from me?" (Psalm 13:1). We ask God to save us, and we are weary from crying out to him, our throats are parched, and our eyes grow dim as we wait for God (Psalm 69:1-3). We cry aloud to God, and we want him to hear us and listen. We try to seek the Lord in our crisis, stretching out our hands but not finding God. Our soul is not comforted. We moan because we are overwhelmed and too distressed to pray. We ask questions that we would not repeat out loud: Has the Lord rejected me forever? Will he never again be kind to me? Is his unfailing love gone forever? Have his promises permanently failed? Has God forgotten to be gracious? Has he slammed the door on his compassion? (see Psalm 77:1-9).

In our confusion we must wait.

It is often at this waiting time we are asked to hold on and we have very little to hold on to. As we wait, faith will grow if we remember. What can we remember? We are creatures who love the great stories of redemption. So much of a growing life of faith requires us to remember. Remember what? Remember the stories

God tells of himself in the Bible. Remember the stories of God's past faithfulness. But at times of great loss and shattered dreams it is difficult to remember. It is for times like these that God gives us others' stories of God's faithfulness. It is at times like this you must borrow someone else's faith because your circumstances do not line up with what you hope is true about God.

My father always told me that there were certain things you should not borrow from your neighbor—money and tools to name just two. However, at times of great struggle, God will often place people in your life and their only purpose is to provide you with a faith from which you can borrow. In the pages that follow, you will read of a deep struggle of faith and life. It is a story of redemption. However, it is presented for you in this form to provide you with a story to borrow from. God may not heal you or answer your prayers in the exact way that he intervenes in this story. Yet, he will give you his presence and will meet you in your struggles. So if life is good as you pick up this journal then celebrate and thank God for your many blessings. Yet remember the story because you may need to borrow from it some day. If, as you pick up this story you are at the end of yourself and feeling broken, read this story and borrow some of this brave women's faith. I am not sure what to say to you as you grieve the losses of your life; however, I am convinced that God is at work to give you the gift of faith. In the meantime, He will send stories like this one from which you may borrow "a cup of faith."

Peace,
Jim Coffield, PhD
Clinical Director
Reformed Theological Seminary

Introduction

My hope in writing this book is that others will find encouragement while trying to stand faithfully in their individual trials. I know firsthand that none of us knows what the future holds. God is the only one who knows the plans he has for each one of us. I know from personal experience that it is so difficult to stand in the middle of the trial. The battleground there is uncertain and difficult terrain. My hope is that you will be reminded that God is greater than your circumstance no matter how bleak it may look at this very moment. His grasp is stronger than your deepest fear and your greatest strife.

I have over these last twenty-four months of my life drawn incredible encouragement from contemporary praise music, especially that of Mark Schultz. I owe God's musicians a debt of gratitude that I can never repay. I encourage you to listen to such music at every opportunity. Our fellowship with the Creator is never closer than at those times when we need him most. While the trials are hard, the memories will hold a sweetness that you will come to cherish once you have overcome your trials. I heard it said once that you will not commend that which you do not cherish. If you can come to the point of cherishing your trial, then you can use your experience to help others God will put in your path. Great Christian literature is another means of encouragement. Find rest and encouragement in the words of great authors like Max Lucado, Charles Swindoll, and the great C.S. Lewis.

Whatever happens to you in your trial and as result of reading my simple words, don't let go of God. Hold tightly to him. He has promised to see you through every circumstance. Focus on his help. Look for it. Cherish it. His promise is that he is with you always even unto the ends of the earth (Matthew 28:20 KJV).

Bebo Norman was one of those whose music encouraged me greatly through this almost unbelievable ordeal. A portion of his song titled, "Borrow Mine" goes like this:

> *You can borrow mine when your hope is gone*
>
> *You can borrow mine when you can't go on*
>
> *Cause the world will not defeat you*
>
> When we're side by side
> *When your faith is hard to find, you can borrow mine*
>
> *You can borrow mine*[1]
>
> Until you are strong again, I have *Faith You Can Borrow.*

Why Me?

God's Providence, Not Ours

I first began to get sick in August of 2005. I was the Information Technology Director for a very large manufacturing facility. I had worked earlier in the week repairing a computer underneath the desk of an employee who was obviously very sick with a nasty sinus-bronchio virus of some sort. It was a very small office environment, and he was spreading all kinds of germs in this little space. Dave coughed with that kind of flem rattling cough that actually made you recoil at the sound of it. I knew my odds of fighting it off were going to be slim. Still, I was optimistic. I was into probiotics and all sorts of health measures, and I washed my hands and used one of those hand sanitizer products. All of this was to no avail though. By the middle of the week, I had awoken early in the morning to the worst head pain I had ever felt. My head felt like it was full of fluid, and I knew I was getting sick. I kept telling myself that a positive attitude could beat anything.

One of my dearest colleagues was scheduled to be in town that day for a visit and I had no intentions of missing a chance to see Troy. By the time he arrived and we managed to squeeze in a bite of lunch, I was praying just to be able to stand up until he left. As soon as he did leave, I walked into my supervisor's office and told her, "Melissa, I am in severe pain. I'm pretty sure I'm getting Dave's infection. I'm going to have to go to the doctor's office. I don't know how Dave managed to stay out of the doctor's office with this. I've never felt such severe sinus pain."

"Well, be careful and call us and let us know what the doctor says," Melissa replied. Halfway to the doctor's office, I phoned my doctor and was instructed to go to the emergency room by my doctor's receptionist. I entered the emergency room and signed in. Less than five minutes later, I began having a severe asthma attack. I was rushed in immediately. Nurses began all sorts of tests. There was a flurry of activity, and questions were being thrown at me at lightening speed. Amid the sights, sounds, and smells that come with the emergency room environment, I was informed that I was very sick and needed to be admitted.

"Mrs. Hickey, we're going to be sending you up to the third floor." I had been given some pain relief medication and managed somehow to slickly talk my way out of being admitted promising religiously to see my primary care doctor the next morning. I'm not even sure of exactly what I said, but I must have been convincing.

I kept my word and went to see my primary care doctor the next morning. He immediately sent me back to the hospital. I was sent to the emergency room again (for insurance reasons) and then admitted. This time, I found out that it was not the worst sinus infection of my life after all. It was a staph infection. My sister Tammarie arrived at the hospital. "I want to know how you got a staph infection!" she demanded.

"I do not know," I replied.

"What kind of staph is it? What is its name?"

"I don't know. They did not tell me." Tammarie's husband had recently passed away due to a bout with MRSA, a severe type of staph infection. Tammarie was quite passionate about the subject and very alarmed at having another relative diagnosed with a staph infection of all things.

I was in the hospital for several days in an attempt to get my white cell count down to a normal range. It took some doing and required the use of antiviral and antibiotic medication given every eight hours. Once released, I was home only a couple of days before the whole cycle started all over again. My doctor once again put me back in the hospital and started the process over. Hourly antibiotic medicines were administered this time in four-hour rounds. Then once I was released, he continued a round of antibiotic and steroid therapies that was beginning to worry the health freak in me. I was also seeing a pulmonologist for the asthma component. He was also concerned about the large amount of steroids being prescribed. I managed to get better for a few days, but then it seemed as though the entire process would start all over again. There seemed to be nothing I could do to beat this cycle.

Since the onset of the infection, I had endured constant and severe facial pain. It felt as though someone were blowing up a soccer ball. It was beyond full and yet the air compressor would not turn off. It was like nothing I had ever encountered before. As the pain would become overwhelming, I would go back to the doctor, and every time I entered the doctor's office, he would send me to the emergency room and tests would start all over.

All of this was having a very negative effect on my job. My boss, a great businessman having built a thriving manufacturing facility that spanned two cities and presently the largest such facility in the state, was not known for his patience. I was under tremendous pressure to get past this. I was fortunate enough to be very skilled at my job and was not in immediate danger of being let go, but the threat was out there.

This latest trip to the emergency room came on the heels of just such a pressure, and I had begun to loathe the ER. The sights, sounds, and smells weighed so heavy on me that I just felt as though I wanted to bolt and run away. I now knew every doctor by name and character type. I was on a first name basis with *all* the nurses. Every entrance to the ER usually meant an eight-hour stay, sometimes followed by admission. This trip I had a very stern doctor, who I called Dr. C. who had begun to get apprehensive about seeing me because of the lack of progress. Dr C. was short in stature and in conversation. After being seen and tested and given pain relief medication, I was asking a nurse to check out and go home. "Excuse me, could you please ask Dr. C. if I could go home? I've been here for several hours, and I need to get home to my kids."

Dr. C. came charging in to tell me, "You are very sick! Do you see this report? You aren't going anywhere!" I tried pleading the *I'm a single mother* case explaining that I needed to get home to care for my two children. Dr. C said very bluntly, "Well, call someone to care for them; you are being admitted." I began to cry uncontrollably. I was fortunate that Dr. C. did not give into my rants, but I could not see that at the time. My white cell count was over 16,000. The nurse on the floor advised me that at 22,000 I would have been at risk for irreversible lung damage!

By now, this whole scenario of my illness had taken weeks and weeks, and I was very frustrated with the medical community. My primary care physician, an extremely sympathetic doctor of Jewish background, was very apprehensive about using pain medication of any kind, and I was in severe pain most of the time. We were making little or no progress against the infection and I was being doused with antibiotics and steroids, which I knew were not good for me. It seemed that in his passion to fix me, he was increasing the use of both antibiotics and steroids. At one point, I was prescribed an oral steroid to take six pills, six times per day. That comes out to thirty-six steroid pills per day in addition to the inhaled steroids I had to take. I was not tolerating the steroids well at all.

I had turned to my dearest and oldest friend during all of this. Doug and I have been friends since we were in diapers, literally. I told him, "I feel as though I am going to die of some hideously unknown ailment."

Doug stated emphatically, "I am not going to let that happen. You're doctor is a knucklehead. Doctors only know how to prescribe drugs." He was determined to help me through this. He began to work diligently with me on natural alternatives. We began using products mixed together and inhaled through a nebulizer to beat the infection.

After a week or so, we were successful and the pulmonologist gave me permission to stop taking the steroids. *Relief at last.* I opted for the diplomatic route of not telling the primary care physician about the natural supplemental treatment. I did however tell him that the pulmonologist took me off the steroids. He frowned. I had obviously annoyed him.

While we had made progress against the infection and for the first time in almost three months and I had a normal white cell count, the facial pain was still present and extreme. More than that, I could feel fluid in my ears, nose, and head. My face was puffy all the time. I swallowed fluid all night most nights. I had gotten to a point of trying sleep in a semi-sitting position because I choked on all the fluid. Laying my head back flat just proved to be too painful. Days and nights dragged on endlessly. I was exhausted from the inability to sleep and wiped out from the constant pain.

My primary care doctor finally agreed to find a specialist. He opted for an ear, nose, and throat specialist. It took over a month to get the appointment. By now it is December of 2005. I had been sick since August. I was not in the office five minutes when the specialist, a very nice and sympathetic gentleman, came in and informed me, "Your case is way out of my area of expertise." I wanted relief so badly from the pain that I simply could not take hearing this. I began to cry. The doctor immediately responded and asked as he handed me a box of tissues, "Why are you so frustrated?"

I told him, "I've been sick since August and my primary care doctor does not believe in the use of pain relief medication *at all,* and I am in so much pain. I can't endure this any longer. You have to be my answer. You just have to be."

He assured me, "I am going to put some wheels into motion immediately. You need to see a neurologist. I am drafting notes, which I want you to take back immediately to your primary care doctor. I am insisting on the use of pain medication." He also wrote a prescription for the pain medication just in case the primary care physician refused to. I did as instructed and took the notes back to the primary care doctor's office, and while my doctor frowned, he proceeded in the direction suggested by the specialist. He asked me if I knew any neurologists in town?

I told him, "I knew a neurologist about ten years ago by the name of Alyn Benezette. I don't know if he even still practices." He put in the call, and I was given an appointment three weeks out. I began to cry again; three more weeks of pain. It would be after the start of the New Year before I would see the neurologist. Months had come and gone and this illness had no face, no name. It was unknown. I did not even know what to tell people was wrong with me.

My boss had now taken me off salary and put me on an hourly wage. He was really frustrated. I knew that I was in danger of losing my position. On top of that, I had a co-worker who was adamant in trying to take over my position with the company. She was not qualified but had a baseline of knowledge and was very pushy. I knew given the right amount of complaining that my boss would give into her demands. Still, I was well liked and knew that there were several key members of the staff who would stand up for me in my continued absence. I was down to working five or six hours per day if at all. My financial situation was becoming serious.

Firm Foundations

In This World You Will Have Trouble

At the time I first began getting sick, I had made a major life decision. I had been part of my church congregation for some fifteen years. However, during that time our church body had grown very large. We had gone from a congregation of a few hundred to a congregation of several thousand. While I knew so many people in our congregation, probably hundreds, I was not getting any response from the body of Christ to my situation. I had begun to become apathetic to attending church. It did not really bother me if I was too tired or not feeling well enough to make it to church on Sunday morning or Wednesday evening. I was not comfortable with that situation. I felt as though it should matter a great deal to me. Frankly, I was also discouraged and scared. I did not understand what was happening to me.

I talked to my friend, Doug. He spoke plainly and clearly and said, "You need to find a new church home. You may not get better soon and having a church family to support you will be very important." He lived several hours away, and while he could offer moral support on the phone, he could not physically be here often to help. I have always thought Doug to be very wise and to have been purposely placed in my life by God to guide me through many things being a single mother causes deficiencies at. So, I took his advice seriously. I got in touch with another long-time friend who had first introduced me to my current church because I knew she and her family were no longer attending there. They had moved to support a son who had gone into ministry and who had become the pastor at another local area church. Gwen immediately had a suggestion. She said that her family was now attending Christ Community Church (CCC) and that I would feel very at home there and she'd love to meet me at one of the services. Prior to even visiting the church, during one of my hospitalizations, two associate pastors from CCC, Matt Walker and Dennis Kiggins came to see me at the hospital at Gwen's request. They prayed with me and asked about my needs; I was shocked by their kindness toward a complete stranger.

A few weeks later, my children were out of town for the weekend so I went to Christ Community Church for Sunday morning service alone. Gwen was right. I immediately was showered with God's love and found myself in tears at the end of the sermon when Senior Pastor Larry Kirk blessed the congregation with a sweet, heart-felt blessing prior to dismissing them. It was not long at all thereafter when the children and I found ourselves looking forward to church once again. Even in pain, I hated to miss a service.

Doug was right (as he usually is). I had no way of foreseeing how sick I would become and having a firm foundation in a strong, loving church made all the difference. God was made very real to my children by the outpouring of love and assistance we received through the months to come through the committed believers at Christ Community Church. They ministered to me every way they could. Suddenly, I had assistance with every emergency room visit. Someone went with me and held my hand every time. When I consider that I made on average two emergency room runs per week, I marvel at what a sacrifice was being made on the part of others! Routinely, people would call me for a grocery list and then just go shopping. Utility bills got paid. Meals showed up frequently. Sometimes, folks would just come and sit with me. Several people helped out with caring for my children. Books or music I made mention of would find their way into my hands.

One of the contemporary Christian songs I hear on the radio

frequently these days talks about the body of Christ and His hands reaching and His feet going. The song is titled *If We Are The Body* and is performed by Casting Crowns. I'm slaughtering the lyrics a little, but my point is that is how it is supposed to work. We are supposed to be his hands and his feet. We are supposed to reach and walk for those who can't do for themselves. This is the fruit of God's love.

Finally, the first of the year came, and I had my appointment with the neurologist, Alyn Benezette. I was surprised to see he now shaved his head; the last time I had seen him, some ten years ago, he had hair. He was as kind as I had remembered him. He was very thorough in his questioning of my history and condition. I immediately felt comfortable that someone with adequate knowledge was working for the betterment of my condition.

He immediately ordered a completely different round of medications that included the use of pain medication and was also very open to my use of natural homeopathic medications. He ordered some tests to verify his suspicions but told me he had a good hunch that I had increased spinal pressure causing a build up of spinal fluid in my head. His questioning led back to the first sign of my illness, the hideous sinus infection.

By the second visit, two weeks later, he had confirmed that he could not find a tumor but had reviewed all the medical reports and stated that he was confident that the staph infection had affected the organ at the base of my brain that produced spinal fluid. He went on to explain that normally our bodies produce exactly enough spinal fluid for us to use up in a twenty-four-hour time period. He needed to perform a spinal tap to obtain a pressure reading. Since no tumor had been found, the only way to confirm for certain the diagnosis of increased spinal pressure would be to perform a spinal tap.

We scheduled it immediately. A normal spinal pressure ranges around the 240 cc mark. A device of tubing and needles is used to create something very similar to a tire pressure gauge which then when tapping the lower end of the spinal column allows you to get this pressure reading. My pressure was 380 cc. My understanding of the condition is that a pressure of 400 puts you in the fatal stroke range. While this whole procedure was very painful, it finally produced an explanation as well as a name for my condition after months of enduring agonizing pain. Medically my condition has two references: Psuedo-Tumor Cerebrai or Benign Inter-cranial Hypertension. Both mean basically the same thing. Pressure is being created in the brain from something other than a tumor.

Dr. Benezette began draining the fluid immediately following the pressure tap and withdrew four vials full of spinal fluid from my brain. The pressure was immediately relieved. Usually this procedure would act as a reset mechanism to the organ that produces the spinal fluid. So we would wait to see if it would be successful in my case. I had the procedure on a Thursday afternoon. I was scheduled to be off work until the following Monday because I had to stay flat on my back following the procedure so as to not cause a leak in the spinal fluid around the spinal cord.

In the meantime, the pushy co-worker had cornered me in my final hours at the office prior to the procedure to tell me that she should be permitted to have my job. I realized that there were only so many battles I could fight. There was to be an impromptu meeting with management to discuss the matter and the impact of my illness on the company. Mary Ellen wanted my support prior to entering the meeting.

"Mary Ellen, I cannot support that decision because it is neither in the best interest of the company nor myself." I also told her, "You are going to have to do whatever you have to do. I am fighting for my life here, and that battle is significantly more important than whether or not I have a job when the tap process is over." It had become clear to me that this illness was draining the life out of me. I also knew that God had gotten me to the point of getting significant medical assistance, and I had to believe that even if I lost this job, something else would be provided. I had survived to this point by no means of my own. After all, I was a single mother of two children whose income had significantly diminished. The world becomes a pretty bleak place when you're a single mother of ten plus years and you realize you cannot provide or care for your children.

The procedure appeared to be successful, and while my neurologist was very sympathetic at having to cause me such pain, we still would have wait to see the end results. I was a model patient and went right home and lay right down. My friend Gwen had come to stay with me following the procedure. Late in the night, near ten o'clock something began to show signs of being desperately wrong. I started shaking uncontrollably from head to toe. I was freezing and despite the piling up of several very thick comforters and quilts, I could not get warm. Gwen called Dr. Benezette who immediately ordered me back to the emergency room. There he ordered medications to calm the symptoms that had mysteriously arisen. The emergency room staff explained, "This type of reaction sometimes occurs due to the extreme reduction of fluid around the spinal cord." After a few hours, I was allowed to return home. Both Gwen and I were exhausted. Sleep finally came for both of us.

The next day just to be cautious, I stayed off my feet for a few additional hours. By four o'clock in the afternoon, I started to show signs of developing fluid in my head and face again. It was not as severe as before (at least at first) but it steadily got worse. By Monday, I was in agony again. Dr. Benezette was startled. He didn't seem to think it was possible for the spinal fluid to have overproduced that much that quickly. However, he was very concerned about my condition and would not rule out the possibility. He cautioned me on the dangers of doing spinal fluid withdrawals in any increments more than once every fourteen days. So we waited. The pain continued and eventually, Dr. Benezette agreed to another tap and withdrawal. Once again, my spinal pressure was very high. This time 360 cc. He expressed his dismay. He sent me home again with strict instructions to stay off my feet.

We had a serious development in the works by my standards. Dr. Benezette was leaving for China for three weeks. His two sons were both missionaries, one in Mongolia, and he had not seen them or his grandchildren in quite some time. I did not want to be the one to deprive him of such a reunion, but I was desperate at the thought of the only person to provide me any relief, leaving the country for almost a month. I felt as though Dr. Benezette was not only my only advocate but also the only person that I had come into contact with who had any understanding of this illness.

Dr. Benezette had ordered the use of narcotic pain relievers, and my primary care physician was very skeptical at this point. On top of that, Dr. Benezette did not use another physician as backup. He used only the hospital for reasons particular to his practice. He assured me that he would leave instructions for his physician's assistant and that the staff would be well informed of my condition. I did honestly try to feel encouraged. I tried not to show my apprehension.

As it turned out, Dr. Benezette attended Christ Community Church so I had the added benefit of seeing him on Sundays if I needed him. This was one of God's many providences in my story. I knew that Dr. Benezette had my best interest at heart, and I tried to be confident that I would survive another three weeks. After all, I had come through everything else.

Dr. Benezette was barely gone when things started to get ugly very quickly. I had gotten to the point where I could no longer stand the pain. I headed to the ER with my trusty sidekick Belinda Shorts, who had quickly become my strength in these times. I was admitted. My primary care physician was called in. I had been placed on a drip of Dilaudid, a narcotic medication eight times stronger than morphine. In addition, I was being given intravenous Phenergren for nausea and Toradol for the inflammation. The Dilaudid was making me sleep most of the time. My primary care physician ordered a pain specialist. He was apprehensive that I was becoming addicted to pain medication and with Dr. Benezette momentarily out of the picture this was his opportunity to invoke his treatment options. Additionally, the hospital ordered another neurologist to come in and review my case since Dr. Benezette was out of the country.

Well, my situation rapidly went from bad to worse. The pain

specialist walked in and took one look at me and ordered additional Dilaudid. The stand-in neurologist questioned the original diagnosis and treatment and the two results combined was all the ammunition my primary care doctor needed to order my immediate discharge. A staff member from the hospital came in and advised me that I was being sent home. She was short, rude, and immediately repeated herself, asking if I could obtain a ride or did she need to call a taxi? Feeling pressured and groggy, I snapped back at her stating, "I can get a ride, but you're going to have to back off long enough to allow me to make a phone call."

I have since that time learned a very important point of medical ethics. Patients have the right to refuse to be discharged. I had been hospitalized for four days at that point on Dilaudid, and even though my primary care physician was recommending the discharge, if I felt that my health was in danger. I had an ethical right to a secondary opinion.

Since that incident, I have run into nurses who vividly remember the the entire sequence of events, which is more than I can do, having been on such heavy medication, and they tell me that they recall being shocked at the discharge. Being dutiful and obedient though, I got a ride home and went there to wait for my neurologist to return from China. There was nothing left at that point but to trust that God would get me through what seemed to be an endless amount of time until Dr. Benezette's return. During the normal business hours that the pain was too severe to handle, I was permitted to go and see Dr. Benezette's physician assistant who was a kind and gentle woman who hated to see me in pain. She would treat me with Toradol injections. The injections might provide me with three to four hours of relief.

Little did I know that more drama was in store for me. I was going to have plenty to keep me busy until Dr. Benezette's return. My primary care physician had withdrawn from my case following the incident at the hospital. He did not even bother to notify me. He instead notified the insurance company who notified Dr. Benezette's office at the next request for a procedure. So there I was in agony with Dr. Benezette in China and no primary care doctor. I felt very much alone.

Many people suggested that I sue the primary doctor. I had neither the energy nor the inclination to do that. My recollection of biblical counsel calls for great caution in the consideration of suiting others. I needed to wisely choose the mountain I wanted to die on, and this was not it. Doug suggested, "This might be the best thing to happen since the whole saga started. Now you can get rid of that knucklehead and get a real doctor." I believe he was right. I quickly learned something important about HMO's—nothing happens without a primary care physician. The whole case stops dead in the water so to speak. Of course, by this time, I had gotten to know plenty of people at the insurance company and knew which cages to rattle and which buttons to push to make sure that they assisted and not hindered in this latest development. Still, making that happen was an incredibly frustrating circumstance.

My father was using a primary care physician by the name of James Brown. He happened to be new in town but was in a medical practice with a physician I knew from my previous church who had always been kind to me. So I used every influence to secure an appointment as quickly as possible. I chose to resist the urge to say everything I thought or felt about the first physician. First of all, God would expect me to show mercy, and secondly, sour grapes might have very likely set a bad tone for my relationship with Dr. Brown.

I was very fortunate. Dr. Brown was very much like a breath of fresh air. He asked me "What went wrong with…Dr. Cohen is it?" I chose to be as diplomatic as possible while also telling him that I felt that the doctor had concerns about my use of pain medication. Diplomacy turned out to be the right tact to use. Dr. Brown was comfortable and offered any assistance he could. He immediately put in a call to Dr. Benezette's office to correlate medication and scheduled a follow up visit following the next scheduled spinal fluid drain.

There were so many times along the way that I had no ability within myself to do anything. I had no strength, no energy, and no relevant knowledge. My only course of action was to rely on God. I had been a Christian entering this trial, but I had never been put through anything like this before in my life. Being a single mother, I had survived divorce. Even the hardship of that experience and the faithfulness of God had not prepared me or so it seemed for what I was walking through at this time. I was only able to take things one hour at a time most days. I know the old saying says "one day at a time," but I did not even have that much strength. I was lost.

I did not understand what was happening to me physically. It seemed for a long time that not even the physician's understood what was happening to me. All I could do was rely on the strength of the Lord. God's people, his musician's and his writers would encourage me. I would hang onto little pieces of encouragement offered through music, sermons, phone calls, and books. Some days, I had to make lists of all the positive things so that all the negative things would not overwhelm me completely. I had to physically count my blessings.

I was constantly questioning the *why* of my situation. What was it that God hoped to accomplish through all this? How would he be glorified through my suffering? Things were spiraling downward quickly financially and physically. There were so many times that I asked the question...*Why Me?* The answer came in the remembrance of part of a sermon I heard at Riverbend Community Church a year or two before. Senior Pastor Roy Hargrave preached the sermon. I don't remember it's title, but I remember him talking about how as Christians we are all either getting ready for a trial, in a trial or just coming out of a trial and if we are not in one of those three places, we should be questioning our walk with the Lord. Then he preached a heart-wrenching sermon on being in the middle of the battle. He talked about some devastating types of trials and how the natural question people ask is *Why Me? Why did this happen?* His response was simple...*Why not me?* God shows mercy to whom he shows mercy. For He says to Moses, "I will have mercy on whomever I will have mercy, and I will have compassion on whomever I will have compassion" (Romans 9:15, NKJV).

By all rights, I am a sinner, and God owes me nothing. The air that I breathe daily is done so by *his* mercy. I am saved by *his* Grace. The words of another sermon also kept coming to my mind. Senior Pastor Bob Coy of Calvary Chapel, Ft. Lauderdale, Florida had preached a sermon I had the privilege of hearing about a year or so before all of this was to begin. The sermon was titled "God is God and You Are Not." There were many times that my friend Doug and I attended Calvary Chapel Ft. Lauderdale together. That was Doug's church of attendance for many years until he moved away from the area. I always treasured getting to attend with him because the sermons were always so unforgettable. I usually left there with deep amazement at the teaching and barely able to speak. This sermon was very moving. The title just sort of says it all. Pastor Bob gave an eloquent study on how God is superior in every way to us as humans. He pointed out the simple point that we don't ever catch God off guard. He is never surprised by anything and he does not ever make mistakes. I had to conclude then that my hideous illness must be ordained and allowed by God and be part of his perfect plan.

I don't want to leave you with the impression that God arbitrarily goes around striking people with illnesses. There are only a few examples of people in the bible being given illnesses specifically for the purpose of glorifying God. The most famous of course is Job. I was no Job by far, although I had friends making the jokes. We are not always privileged to know why God does what he does. "'For My thoughts are not your thoughts, Nor are your ways My ways.' Declares the Lord" (Isaiah 55:8, NAS). Steven Curtis Chapman has a song titled *Believe Me Now* that says that God never wastes a single hurt that we go through.[1] I believe that is firmly true. God is orderly and merciful and full of love. While he is just and will ultimately punish the wicked, he does not go around senselessly hurting people. Knowing this and being able to trust that he knows more than I ever will, allowed me to struggle in faith.

Yes, that's right, *struggle in faith*. Like Jacob, I wrestled with God but in that desperate way of needing to hang on to him as Jacob did that night sleeping near the rock. Clinging to the only thing that made sense in a world that had gone senseless for me. In this world, you will have troubles. Make no mistake about that precious one. Having a firm foundation gives you the ability to stand in the face of trials and trouble. The winds of change are often hurricane force winds. Without a firm foundation, your house will be the one that gets flattened.

Understanding Your Trial

You may not know why you are walking through your trial. I certainly did not. But you can be confident that your trial has purpose. This does not mean that you are not meant to feel pain and suffering. You are also as a Christian, not meant to brush it away or stow it some place where it cannot be seen. We have no way of knowing how other lives will be touched by what they watch us go through. We suffer with hope. We have the ultimate hope that Christ has overcome the world and thereby every evil thing including sickness and death. As a Christian and because of this hope, we do not suffer as the world suffers. The world's agony has no point and rarely a positive end. God promises however, "...that all things work together for good to those who love God, to those who are the called according to his purpose" **(Romans 8:27-29).**

There were times along my journey that I broke down and questioned God with great sincerity. I went to see the Associate Pastor at my church, Matt Walker, several times (usually in tears) when the trials would seem to get harder than I could bear. He reminded me that David, considered a man after God's own heart, often cried out in his agony to God. I thought of how as a parent, I am most touched when my children share their greatest frustrations with me. I know they really trust me when they share their really personal hurts with me. How much greater that must be for our Heavenly Father. How close he must feel to us when we break down and share those intimacies with him.

On one of my questioning/counseling sessions with Pastor Matt,

I remember crying and telling him that I need that God that is larger than life to reach down and touch me, the one who left heaven and gave up deity to become a mortal man so that he could reach out and touch the woman at the well. I need *that* God who was willing to bridge *that* gap. Pastor Matt gave me a copy of Dr. Philip Yancey's book, *Where Is God When It Hurts*.

Dr. Yancey has done a tremendous amount of research on pain and its origins. He has done a lot of work with leper colonies here in the United States and abroad and some of his findings are amazing.

Dr. Yancey describes how pain is a part of God's design to help as a warning system for the body. He has also shown that lepers do not lose their fingers and toes because of the disease of leprosy but because of the hazards they encounter from not being able to feel pain in their fingers and toes.[1]

Pain serves a purpose in our lives. Your pain has a purpose. Even if you never get the answer to the *why?* of your trial this side of heaven, keep seeking out God's purpose. Seeking out God's purpose makes bearing your trial easier. It also shifts your focus to God and takes the focus off of you. Max Lucado (my favorite author of all time) expresses the idea in his book, *Facing Your Giants* that when you focus on God your giant stumbles. When you focus on your giant, *you* stumble. So don't suffer as the world does, *suffer with hope*.[2]

Focus on God and let your giant stumble. Allow God to use your trial to help others. I promise as one who has walked in the path of trials and trouble that he will do just that.

My physical condition continued in the pattern of spinal fluid drains and pressure refilling my head less than forty-eight hours later. By now, I had the whole cycle down to a precise science. Theoretically, the first spinal fluid drain should have acted as a reset button to the organ that produces spinal fluid. In my case, as I can do nothing normal, that seemed to not be the case. By the fourth drain, I had developed one of those spinal fluid leaks following the procedure and had to have a secondary procedure called a spinal blood patch to fix the leak. My back was much like a pincushion by this point. How this procedure works is that they take some blood out of your arm and put it back into your spine near the point of the drain, and it sort of acts like putty and covers the leak. While that may not sound too difficult, it is much more painful than the original spinal fluid drain.

Doug had come up for this procedure. He had not been here for the previous procedures and was really starting to worry about me. Doug's mom, one of the most kind and gentle people I had ever met, had passed away a few years earlier from brain cancer. My illness was hitting a little too close to home for Doug. I did not know how significant that was at the time. Doug told one bad joke after another in the pre-op area. He kept me giggling so as to not let me get apprehensive. Doug was very often just good for my soul. The nurse came out and said that it was time. She introduced herself to Doug and assured him that I would be fine. She gave him one final instruction. "Give her a kiss so we can take her away. I promise we'll bring her back." Doug bent over and gently kissed my cheek. Doug and I were neither one prone to showing much emotion around other people. I knew it made him uncomfortable, but he was obedient.

I smiled and said, "Wait right here. I want to see you when I get out. Pray for me."

Because I had endured four of the procedures already, the anesteologist had a terrible time getting the needle into my spine I cried through the whole procedure, and unfortunately, they cannot put you to sleep for this procedure because they need feedback from you so as to not push blood into your brain.

When it was all over Doug asked, "How did it go?" He could see my tear stained face.

"I'm glad it is over." I replied.

"I cried through the whole thing."

"Did you really?" Doug asked.

"Yes. It hurt that bad. Doug, I don't think I can do this anymore."

"Well, lets get you home. You're past it now. It's over." Doug said.

"Yes, but for how long?" I responded without thinking. In between spinal fluid drains, I would live in the emergency room. I made on average two trips per week. This was no kind of life. I had walked out of work about two months earlier planning on being out for four days and had so far been unable to return. My emotional condition was taking as much of a beating as my physical condition. I had time to conduct quite a bit of research on Psuedo-Tumor Cerebrai. No scientific/medical explanation exists as to why this condition originates. The cause of the condition is considered unknown. There was also no known cure. There were few treatment options available and those did not seem to have great success. I had read hundreds of stories of Psuedo-Tumor patients who had pursued repeated treatment options with no cure. Some had been able to manage the disease but I had not found one that had been able to recover from it. I could not imagine living in this kind of physical state.

At this point, Dr. Benezette was desperately trying to obtain a neurosurgeon. We needed to find another alternative to our present course of treatment. But we were having troubles on this front. I could not continue to have fluid build up and drained off only to have to repeat the process every fourteen days. There were only three neurosurgeons in the Daytona Beach area, and all of them had a minimum six-month wait for new patients no matter how severe the diagnosis. Dr. Benezette made personal calls, as did I, and we were unable to budge schedules. The only way I could be seen in less than six months was to have a stroke as a result of the condition.

Dr. Benezette felt that the next move might be to install a brain shunt, which would drain the fluid off constantly. He said that it was not likely that any surgeon would try to do more than that at this time since the diagnosis was pseudo-tumor—meaning no tumor had been found. Most doctors would feel that the problem was too large to actually resolve. It would be like looking for a needle in a haystack.

I could not seem to go longer than fourteen days without a spinal fluid drain. It took a lot of prayer and faith to get me to show up for each drain knowing how much pain I was going to endure. Dr.

Benezette would smile each time and say, "I am proud of you Annie. You're a real trooper!"

I would reply, "Yes, and you are my Hero!" I would take the immense pain of a spinal tap procedure for just a few precious hours of relief. If I were an extremely good patient, I could get thirty-six to forty-eight hours of relief from the drain, never a minute more. As in the emergency room, I knew all the nurses in same day surgery by face and name.

On one occasion when no one could go with me for one of the procedures and I was feeling very alone, I was surprised to see a nurse there, Meg Iglesias, who I had gone to church with for many years. I had not even known she worked there. She did not know that I was no longer attending my former church.

"I saw your name on the patient roster for today. What is going on with you?" Meg asked with concern.

I responded, "Well, I've been pretty sick for a few months. I have a condition called Psuedo Tumor Cerebrai."

"How did you get sick?" Meg asked.

"We're not really sure. We think it started with a staph infection."

"Are you scared?" she wanted to know.

"Yes. I've had the procedure before, but it's very painful, and I'm never quite sure that I can get through the next one. It takes everything I have just to show up." She prayed with me and even was permitted to stand in for the procedure.

God made sure that my needs for personal contact were met even then. There was no debate over my need. God just met me where I was as He had done so many times before quietly and without fanfare. God will meet you where you are too. Mark Schultz has a song that I just love. It talks about how God loves you right where you are and you will know it when you are back in his arms again. The song is titled "Back in His Arms."[3]

Mark Schultz came to Daytona Beach at the end of March to perform in a benefit concert for our local Christian radio station. I have a friend who happens to be a nurse. She and I have been friends for many years now. My friend Laura and I often attended concerts together whenever we could. However, I rarely went anywhere those days—except maybe to church. Laura knew I was sick and had called about the concert.

"I don't think I could sit up for that long," I told Laura on the phone.

"I refuse to let you miss this!" she replied. "I am coming by at five thirty with my boyfriend, Tony, and I'll make sure that you can endure this. Do you have medication for pain?"

"Yes", I replied, "but I don't want to put you to any trouble."

Laura quickly responded, "It's no trouble at all. We'll see you in a little while." She came along with the new beau she was dating (whom she would eventually marry) and after making sure I had been properly medicated to endure the concert, they loaded me up and hauled me off to the auditorium. This was my first experience with a Mark Schultz concert. I was only familiar with one of his songs that had been written years earlier when my son was just a baby. Mark had released a song the year my son was born. It was titled, "He's My Son."[4] The song tells the story of a prayer being prayed by a parent of a very sick child. I knew the song very well because I sang it to my son often. My son had been born very ill with a condition, which required us to spend most of our time during his first two years in emergency rooms and pediatric intensive care units. Mark originally wrote the song about a young man in his youth group that had been diagnosed with Lukemia. The song however, perfectly applied to my little man. It was my prayer on so many occasions, especially when my son's condition was critical. I was thrilled to be going to hear Mark in a live concert. I was hoping he would sing the song. I marveled at the timing of this concert and how the situation had been reversed and now I was the one needing the prayer of that song. I don't think that words can express how much Mark's music lifted my spirits that night. It seemed even though there was an auditorium full of fans, that the only people in the room were myself, Mark, and God. I felt for an all too brief time that God came down and kissed my forehead and said everything will be okay—not necessarily that I would recover but that it would all be ok.

Mark's special gift in music is helping his audience face really difficult circumstances. He is not afraid to sing about the issues that break our hearts. He does it in such a way that his songs offer great hope. When it was all over, I knew that I needed to have that kind of encouragement more often. Despite my very bleak financial situation, I somehow had enough money in my pocket that night to purchase a CD/DVD combination, which Mark was selling for ten dollars. I wore that DVD out over time. My son came home the next day and we sat on the couch and watched the DVD together. When we got up to the place in the DVD where Mark sings "He's My Son," I paused the DVD and told Justin how I used to sing this song to him in intensive care. I then resumed the DVD. When it was over, Justin had tears streaming down his face and very quietly looked up at me whispered, "Play it again, Mommy." You may be presented with an opportunity to help someone in such a manner. Don't miss it. Laura will never know this side of heaven how much encouragement that one night kept on giving me for months to come and still does. It might not have been a big thing to her but it was everything to me.

A few days after this, around the first of April, Dr. Benezette's office called to say that a neurosurgeon at Shands Hospital at the University of Florida in Gainesville, Florida had agreed to see me. Dr. Benezette had made a personal request. I was to go up May 4 and meet with a Dr. Richter. May 4 seemed like an eternity away. I immediately called and made an introduction and begged for an earlier appointment. A very kind receptionist informed me, "Unfortunately, there just aren't any other appointment times available for new patients." The receptionist felt touched by my story and promised to put me on a cancellation list. That was at least something. Although, I knew by now that the odds of someone canceling a long-awaited appointment with an in-demand neurosurgeon was not likely. I refused to lose hope though. God would either get me to the appointment or get me there sooner. I called twice a week to check on the cancellation list. I realize that sounds a bit pesky, but I had also learned by now that really good doctor's offices get very busy very fast; you might get pushed down in the pile by virtue of overload.

I had managed to get in touch with a lifetime friend from high school Selina Surles who lived in the Gainesville area. I had not spoken with her for a couple of years because I had lost her number. It wasn't long before we were up to speed, and she was prepped for my upcoming visit. My sister decided to make the two-hour drive with me to meet the neurosurgeon. This was to be an introductory appointment, but she had plenty of questions. I knew she would be thorough in her questioning. I knew she would be looking out for me. I was tired and worn out and in pain. Having someone else looking out for you in that circumstance is of great comfort.

We arrived at the Department of Neurosurgery at Shands Hospital. We checked in and sat down to wait. My head had been cooking pretty well for the last half an hour or so.

"Tam, I need to find a restroom. I think I'm going to be sick," I said with some urgency.

"Okay, hang on," she said then asked as to its location.

I went to the restroom and passed out. The next thing I remember, I was being whisked into an exam room and given moist towels and my sister (a very humorous person) was cracking jokes once she was assured I was okay. The neurosurgeon made an appearance almost immediately. I was expecting a longer wait.

He immediately announced, "We're going to admit you. You'll be taken down after that for some tests. I anticipate that we will operate sometime tomorrow depending on the trauma schedule." My sister and I looked at each other and then back at him in shock.

I stumbled over a few words. "We did not come prepared for a stay. I don't have anyone scheduled to watch my kids for that long a time period."

He said rather frankly, "I did not book this appointment expecting you to pass out in my waiting area either. You obviously have a tremendous amount of pressure building up, and I think it is in your best interest for us to try and relieve it." He was ordering some immediate tests, and surgery would be scheduled as available between emergencies and the existing schedule for the following day.

There was suddenly much to do and very little time to do it in. I had to see an ophthalmologist. This particular diagnosis is considered life threatening when pressure builds up on the optic nerve(s). An exact level of optic nerve pressure had to be obtained for that purpose. A CT scan had to be obtained as well as x-rays to determine if there was enough space in the ventricle of the brain to install the shunt. I had been given a choice of three shunt procedures to choose from. One procedure involved going in through the optic area. I still shudder at the description of that one. The second procedure while the easiest also had the highest risk of failure due to the shunt becoming dislodged later. It involved installing the shunt in the lower end of the spinal cord. One good sneeze or one bad bend could have dislodged that.

The third choice (and the one my sister and I settled on) was termed a VP Shunt procedure. It involved opening the skull and entering the brain area and installing a shunt in the left or right ventricle of the brain. From there, it would extend down the back of the throat, through the chest, and end up in the peritoneal cavity where spinal fluid would be deposited allowing it to be absorbed by the body tissue and processed like any other food product. Spinal fluid is made up mostly of water and proteins so the body tissues can absorb it.

Things had begun to move so quickly. I barely had time to think now. I had kind nurses and medical students (Shands is a teaching hospital), and they were doing all they could to make me comfortable. My folks with my kids were on their way.

"Annie, I think I'm going to head back if you are settled," my sister announced. She disliked hospitals very much. My friend Selina was coming over. Everything now was hurry up and wait. I sent my dad down with my kids to purchase something to wear on my head after the surgery from the hospital gift shop. My children had never seen me without hair, and I had serious concerns about how that would affect them. Selina brought pajamas and socks since we had not come prepared for an overnight stay. (By now, I knew one thing that really helped to alleviate the stress caused by the hospital environment was being able to wear normal pajamas instead of those awful hospital gowns.)Shands Hospital was used to dealing with very long term sick people and was more than willing to accommodate me in that request. In order to really appreciate the somewhat chaotic scene that was taking place, I need to add the detail that my mother, now in her mid seventies had been suffering with Alzheimer's disease for over five years. She asked about every five minutes or so why everyone was gathered together. We would all chuckle and explain that I was going to have brain surgery. She would look shocked and dismayed. She would then ask why, and we would go through the brief explanation all over again. Every time she would realize Selina was in the room, she would coo with excitement and ask her all about her dad and her husband and did she have any kids. There was plenty to distract me from the nervousness of the moment.

As the evening settled, Pastor Matt called to pray with me and wish me well—faithful Pastor Matt. There is sometimes nothing as comforting as that prayer from a trusted counselor of God, someone you know spends his life in God's presence. Pastor Matt's wife Renee had a similar condition to mine (another one of God's providences) so we had bonded very early on. I knew they were genuinely pulling for me and waiting with baited breath to see how things would turn out as much for Renee's sake as for mine. Renee had her condition longer than me, but at the time my surgery was taking place, had not made it to the point of being referred to a surgeon. Her spinal fluid drains were more successful than mine.

It was finally time. The children and I said our good-byes. "Listen, please do not worry. Remember everything that Mommy has told you. God will take care of me. He has brought us this far. Remember, no matter what happens, God does not make mistakes. No matter where things go from here, remember that Mommy loves you very much and God loves you even more." It took everything I had to choke back and not appear teary eyed. I could not let them see that. I knew they needed strength and reassurance. The sudden realization that anything can happen in the operating room loomed over us all like a heavy blanket of smoke. I did my best to assure Cassidy and Justin that God would take care of me and no matter what happened next, God did not make mistakes.

My dad, a man who rarely was prone to showing mushy emotion leaned over and said, "Try not worry. We love you and you will be just fine. I know it." I went into pre-op and was given some final instructions before being given the anesthesia. Very soon I was out.

Do Everything You Can

Recognize Your Limits

I was awoken from the anesthesia. I felt very out of control. I didn't handle the whole matter well at all. I was really hysterical. The nurse had to call Doug on the phone. He had not been able to get there on such short notice, and I was terrified at having to go through this without my shield of confidence being there. "Please, I need to speak to him. I am in so much pain," I frantically reasoned. I couldn't find the phone.

"Calm down, Annie. You're fine. You've had surgery," the nurse tried to explain.

"He couldn't be here. I need him." I thrashed about on the gurney as I replied.

"Okay, I'll get him on the phone. What is his number?" The nurse gave up in frustration.

"He's number two on speed dial, but I can't find the phone. I need to talk to Doug." I could not seem to reason anything as the tears flowed from my eyes. The nurse placed the phone in my hand. "Here he is. Talk to him." she said.

"Doug? Are you there?" I asked in desperation.

"Yes, I am here. How do you feel?" he asked.

"I am in so much pain," I replied.

"They are going to give you something for that. You made it through, kid. Everything went very well the nurse said. You're going to be well in no time." Doug tried to be reassuring. I couldn't stop crying.

It wasn't long before I was taken back to my room. I was told the surgery had been successful. Prior to entering the operating room, Dr. Richter had let me know that my ventricles were small, and while he thought he would be successful, he had some concerns that the ventricle would collapse forcing him to try a second ventricle. We had been lucky and that had not happened.

Selina was the first to see me, but not before I had gotten a hold of a mirror. I had awoken to find half of my hair gone, shaved off right down the middle of my head. The other half was a matted, bloody mess. I had no idea what to do with it. Not to mention, I was trying to work around staples, stitches, and bandages. Selina, not being squeamish at all (lucky for me), gave it a whirl. "I can't believe they don't clean up any of this, Ann. It's one big matt of blood and goo," Selina said. "Am I hurting you?" she wondered cautiously. She was somewhat frustrated that they did not clean up their work a little more.

A nurse who happened to overhear the grumbling chimed in, "they are doctors, nothing more." My head was very sore, and Selina was not able to make very much progress. My dad came in next, and we attempted to put on the items he had purchased to cover my head. One had elastic in it and was just too painful and made me look like Little Bo Peep, but I wanted so much to see my children. The other option was a shower cap. My father was a great man but not a great shopper. I opted for the pain of the elastic. They came in, and I was so overjoyed at one more chance to hug my children. They visited until I could stand the pain no longer. Then I asked them to leave so Mommy could remove the cover from my head. The nurse came by shortly thereafter with some painkiller.

I could not feel the tube in my head or in the rest of me. Dr. Richter came in to my room. "The surgery went better than we anticipated. Your ventricles held up well. As soon as we are certain that everything is okay, we're going to let you go home." Given my financial situation, I asked about going back to work. He said, "I'd like you to give it thirty days."

"Could I possibly negotiate two weeks?" I asked cautiously.

He said, "I'll leave that up to your neurologist." I agreed. The following day I was allowed to leave the hospital. My dad, mom, and the kids were glad that I was coming home.

I saw Dr. Benezette fairly quickly following the surgery. Seven days following the surgery, he was required to remove the staples and stitches. Because the tube ends in the peritoneal cavity, there were staples in my abdominal area as well as in my head.

Almost immediately, we began having problems with the lower end of the shunt. It began to show signs of rejection. Dr. Benezette had warned me prior to the surgery that such was a possibility. I contacted the neurosurgeon's office and was told that rejection was highly unlikely. I went back to Dr. Benezette needing help—quickly! He immediately started me on medication to offset the rejection. My children and I came to call this medication the "Crazy Pills." I could be known to walk into walls after taking it. It made me completely physically and emotionally unstable. We were not successful in getting things under control and within a week or so, I found myself signing into the emergency room with shunt complications.

I found out quickly that there was a downside to having a shunt put in two hours away from where I lived. Local facilities did not want to touch someone else's work—especially not something so critical— and two hours is a long way to drive to go to the emergency room. Dr. Benezette ordered in some traditional medication but was at a loss to do anything more. The emergency room attending physician called Dr. Richter and demanded that he do something. Dr. Richter agreed to have me come back up to Shands the following week.

Before that could happen, my head had again begun to fill with fluid. I knew the symptoms all too well. I fought it off as best as I could. I prayed faithfully. I called everyone I knew and asked them to pray. Nothing seemed to help. By Sunday, I had called Dr. Benezette. He agreed to meet me late in the afternoon at the emergency room for what was to be my ninth spinal fluid drain.

"This is an extremely risky procedure once a shunt is in place.

Remove too much fluid and you could cause permanent paralysis or death," Dr. Benezette explained.

I asked him to continue. "Let's do this thing. I am in too much pain. I don't know anyone else I'd trust with my life," I explained. Following this procedure and the high pressure of the fluid, Dr. Benezette informed Dr. Richter that something was wrong with the shunt and that it was very likely that a second shunt was going to have to be installed. I got ready to head back to Gainesville. May 5 had been the date of the first brain surgery; we were only now heading into the Memorial Day Holiday at the end of May.

Dr. Richter immediately put me on the waiting list for surgery for the following day, Thursday. We waited some eight hours to be put in for a surgical slot. Once in pre-op, Dr. Richter informs me, "I will wait until I get into the OR to determine my final course of action, but I want you to know that I am considering a shunt revision." This news was upsetting to me as I was expecting to obtain a second shunt or the very least a new shunt.

"I don't understand. What is a shunt revision?" I nervously asked.

Dr. Richter explained, "A shunt revision is where we go in and try to repair the shunt rather than replace it. We may be able to ascertain the cause of the blockage or other issue. If we can't do that, I'll look at what our best option is. You'll already be sedated so I won't be able to get your permission once you're under anesthesia. I'll need you to agree to this now and sign off on it."

I had not come into this circumstance in nearly as good a form as I had the previous surgical procedure. My hopes were being sorely tested.

On top of everything, my life-long friendship with Doug seemed to become strained beyond imaginable limits. I had called Doug to inform him of the latest development. "Will you go with me to Shands for the surgery? I did not do so well without you last time." I was genuinely shocked at his response. It was full of frustration and anger and bitterness.

"You know, you have been so sick for so long...What is it that you expect me to do at Shands? I am not a brain surgeon! Am I supposed to give up my weekend with my kids for this and drive four hours?" Doug was a single parent who shared custody of his kids with his ex-wife. I had never heard such bitterness in Doug's voice before. I reeled at the words. I was so crushed that I could hardly speak. It was as if someone had kicked me in the stomach.

It was the start of a long trial of its own, and I was emotionally devastated. Doug had always been my special and vivid reminder of heaven and God's gracious mercy. Now it was clear he was genuinely angry. I did not understand why. It was not even possible for me to understand why he was angry given my present physical state. It would be months later before that answer would come. Still, I had to go forward. Selina also was not going to be able to get to Shands prior to the surgery—especially since we weren't sure exactly when that surgery was going to be. She was helping another friend in serious need, and I did not feel as though I could pull her off that duty. She would try to come over after the surgery. So, I was going into this one with just my folks and the kids. My friend Joyce had given me a ride to the hospital and had waited a while in pre-op. She would become a regular rider with me to Shands in future months. She was great company.

I said my good-byes once again after a very long wait and headed off for brain surgery number two. This brings us back to the upsetting news of the possibility of not getting a second shunt or even a new shunt. Seeing that I was highly upset and not wanting to put me under anesthesia that way, Dr. Richter assured me that the problems could all be at the bottom of the tube and it might not be necessary to remove the whole thing. He further reminded me that my ventricles were small to start with, and he was asking for trouble by going into them a second time. "If they collapse, I'll have even worse problems on my hands." He also said, "This time I am taking additional measures by adding a secondary procedure, whereby I'll wake you up post-operatively and take you to ICU. I'll put you back to sleep there, drill a hole in your head, and insert an external tube that will allow us to monitor pressure twenty-four hours per day for several days in Intensive Care."

This might sound encouraging to the average patient but to me it just caused more tears. I had not had to be in Intensive Care during the first surgery. To me, the Intensive Care Unit was the sign of doom. Seeing that he was not making much progress with me, he opted for a more diplomatic route. "Annie, the entire neurosurgical department met and discussed your case prior to your arrival. Very smart people have helped to develop this care plan." What choice did I have? Let him try or go home and die? There did not seem to be much choice. I thanked him for his efforts, signed all the necessary forms, and they administered the anesthesia.

I awoke this time much more subdued than after the previous surgery. Dr. Richter told me, "We corrected a blockage at the bottom end of the tube that we hope corrects this problem. We will proceed with taking you to ICU where we will put you back to sleep and drill the hole for the monitoring tube." I was fairly groggy and very unarguementative.

I had returned home after the first surgery with half my hair. Once all of the matted mess was removed, there was nothing left to do but shave it off. My other option would have been to go around looking like a forty-one-year-old punk rocker want-a-be. I opted to shave it off and start clean. My one positive outlook at the end of the second surgery was having narrowly escaped having to have it all shaved off again as it was barely half an inch long at that point. That joy was very short lived. Once in ICU, the excited young neurosurgical medical students that I was getting to know entirely too well informed me apologetically that they were going to have to shave my head again. They were apologetic because as they put it, "We're not barbers." They were excited because this procedure was not one they performed all that often. (I think they were drawing straws over who got to drill the hole through my skull and insert the tube.) Very shortly, the lights went out again. Off to sleep I went.

I was awoken a short time later and told that the procedure went very well. I felt like I was all tied up. I felt like I could not move. The tube in my head was very small but linked up over my pillows to a television monitor that displayed the pressure in my head. I had really great nurses in ICU. Every time I got that tangled up feeling, they would very patiently come and move the tube. It usually got tucked between the pillow and the mattress. The critical care unit I was in was one of several at Shands and must have been serious because I was the only fully conscious patient in the ward. I think I was only one of six patients in the entire ward for two nurses. While I was also the only fully ambulatory patient, I was not permitted to get up and go anywhere because the tube was attached to the monitor and could not be unattached. No one was permitted in to see me, but I did not know that little detail. I was kept fairly well medicated, which was a good thing.

While my cell phone actually worked in the ward, only one nurse would allow me to turn it on. The rest insisted that I keep it off. After the first twenty-four-hour period, I began to suffer from a syndrome that one of the nurses explained to me later was common for those patients placed in ICU wards who were fully conscious. It was produced by a lack of contact and interaction. After forty-eight hours in the ICU ward, I asked a nurse if they would call Selina. I did not understand why she had not come. I reached Selina's voice mail and left a message for her to call the ICU ward. I tried again on the next shift with the same results. On the third day, I was really becoming a basket case. I missed my kids horribly. I felt alone and had very little encouragement. On top of that, I was not feeling all that great, and yet I had that sinking feeling that everything was showing normal on the charts.

Early on the fourth morning, Dr. Richter came in with his team of students and said, "We have monitored the pressure for four days and it has not once gone above normal. We feel that our work has been a success. Would you like to go home?" By this time, I was really not feeling well and there was definitely pressure in my head although it was minimal.

I tried explaining this. He began to get frustrated. "Dr. Richter, I'm never wrong about these things," I insisted. The one thing I knew with all my might was that he could not send me home to go back to the kind of existence I had endured for months. I had sacrificed everything to have a shot a normal life. I had no intentions of leaving without it. In my opinion, he wasn't offering much proof that I was going to get my shot. Dr. Richter very kindly said, "You're stepping out of your league. You are also insulting my work. I'm going to go ahead and discharge you today. Can someone come and get you?" He then tried to encourage me to give it some time. "Annie, I tried telling you the first time we met that your expectations may be too high. This may be as good as it gets. Psuedo Tumor patients rarely get better."

I told him politely, "Dr Richter, your expectations are way too low."

The students took the tube out of my head and asked me if I wanted anesthesia to stitch it up. "Why wouldn't I?" I asked. I was given an explanation about how the anesthesia is a local and the application hurts more than the stitches. (I should have disregarded that story.) I opted not to get the anesthesia. I cried and I hollered ouch several times. I could not wait for them to finish. My very nice nurse told me that med students always give bad advice like that because they've never had anyone stitching up a hole in their skull before. "Why didn't you interject and help me out before I let them proceed?" I asked.

He replied, "Nurses rank below med students." I understood. A few moments later the nurse answered the phone and said, "Selina is on the line. Do you want to talk to her?" Selina had a desperate tone in her voice. "Ann, I've been trying to get through to you for four days! When someone is in ICU at Shands they might as well be in Fort Knox." She had my PIN number that the hospital uses for accessing secure information about patients. She was chewed out by somebody for having it because she was not immediate family.

I told her, "I am being discharged. I am waiting on Dad to come and pick me up." I also told her, "I am not feeling very well either."

She said, "Call the administrator." I had been the protest route before, and I was frankly afraid that if things went badly, I'd have no one to treat me. So I opted to be meek and trust that God had not been surprised by this turn of events.

I turned on my cell phone to find half a dozen messages or so from Doug to my utter shock and dismay. I had not expected to hear from him considering our last conversation. They were all kind, and I listened and saved them to listen to later; I chose not to call him back. I thought it best under the circumstances of the conversation we had prior to the surgery for me to let things be. I said a quiet prayer of thankfulness but did not return the calls. Shortly thereafter, Dad and my kids arrived with Grandma in tow, and we all headed home a second time. This time, I had ample soft scarves to cover my head with. Ten minutes or so into the ride home, it was apparent that I was running a fever. Not at all shocking after such a procedure. However, between Gainesville and Daytona Beach lies the Ocala National Forest and absolutely zero cell phone reception. So it was almost two hours before we could get in touch with either Shands or Dr. Benezette to let them know of the fever. In the meantime, I started Advil. Shands had advised me to continue the Advil or Motrin. I was told I could have Tylenol alternating every two hours, and if it did not clear up, I was to come back up to their emergency room. Dr. Benezette said the same. I took a pain pill, a nausea pill, two Motrin and went to bed upon arriving home. My hopes had been sorely tested.

I would not exactly say that I had run the good race. I'm not sure that the Apostle Paul would have been at all impressed. I think the best that I could say at this point was that I was still hanging in there. It wasn't by much and I was feeling pretty defeated, but I was still there. I had pressure behind my eyes and in my head. I was sick to my stomach.

I had managed to alienate my surgeon and my best friend. Worst of all, I had no hope at all that this ordeal was over. It could be said that I had every right to doubt. I think that was understandable given my circumstances. Doubting I think is inevitable for most of us. What is important is to deal with doubt the right way. Deal with disbelief or disappointment of your circumstance in the right way. Don't hide your doubt away. Don't pretend it doesn't exist. Don't use it as an excuse to count on your own ways or your own abilities. One can be wise even with doubt. I had much to doubt at this point. Was I going to ever be well? Was I going to lose my oldest and dearest friend in the world? Was I going to lose my job? Was I going to lose my Home? Would I lose my surgeon? Would I after going through all of this...lose my life?

So what do you do with doubt? How do you handle it wisely? You share your doubt first with God and then with your Christian community. Seek wise counsel. God's grace is in the midst of honest doubt. The issue is who God is—not who you are. There are two great weapons against doubt: information and faith. Find out all you can. "Study to show thyself approved unto God, a workman that needeth not to be ashamed, rightly dividing the word of truth" (2 Timothy 2:15, KJV). Know your limits. Know where your work ends and God's begins. God is made strong in our weakness.

But he said to me, "My grace is sufficient for you, for my power is made perfect in weakness." Therefore I will boast all the more gladly about my weaknesses, so that Christ's power may rest on me.

2 Corinthians 12:8-9

There is no way to arrange the Christian life that you don't have to have a radical faith. Our life is lived by faith in God who is a gardener at work in our lives. He tends the vines of our lives with love and great skill. Draw your strength and comfort in him. It's okay to grieve and to doubt but let that grief and doubt draw you back to the one who can give you life. "I am the vine; you are the branches. If a man remains in me and I in him, he will bear much fruit; apart from me you can do nothing" (John 15:5, NIV).

The Trials in The Middle

oing through two brain surgeries and an agonizing illness would have been enough by itself for any one person let alone any one Christian to endure. There were lots of other non-medical trials going on in the middle of all of this that added to the pressure put on me.

There was my financial situation. Having gone from earning a regular weekly income to having had little or no income had all but devastated us financially. Several times throughout the course of these events, people who cared suggested that I meet with one of the church elders who specialized in finance, Blake Thomas. Always, I politely declined. The church was never insistent. They were patient. I declined because I felt that I had nothing to work with at that point. It wasn't like I was running up credit card debt. I had little or no existing debt prior to getting sick. I owned my vehicle outright, a small SUV. I had purchased it and paid for it in a period of six months. I only possessed one credit card for Sears with a $250 balance on it at the time. It also wasn't like I had any means of taking a second job. I was very sick. I was a single mother, a working white woman whom the government would not assist because I generally earned too much money. I did not qualify for unemployment or disability. I also allowed unpleasant experiences at my former church to cloud my judgment in this situation. I was afraid of being put down for not being an adequate provider. I might have fared better had I sought out some of that advice. If you find yourself in a situation where finances overwhelm you, the best thing you can do is to turn to someone who can look objectively at your situation and see all the alternatives that due to stress you may not be able to see yourself. Ignoring your financial situation will not help to make it one bit better.

I also had the very real trial of failing parenthood—at least I felt as though I was failing parenthood. I had become physically unable to help my children with anything, including the basics of food preparation, daily living activities, or homework. Most nights they did not even stay at my home. I missed them terribly but was unable to tolerate having them near for more than just a few minutes because I felt so compelled to be a mom that it wore me out physically. I had long-time, great friends who stepped in to help when asked. It took more than one family to help juggle and to try and help my children maintain some form of a normal life. I was also struggling with the future. I had to face the very real possibility that I might not survive this awful illness. Everyday that we went on without successfully resolving my illness had made that more apparent. I had to make arrangements for who would care for my children and for what resources I had available to assist with that. I had to help my children face the possibilities. No matter what happened, I wanted them to know that God does not make mistakes. I can think of no greater sobering moment in my life than when I made the phone call to speak with my long-time friend Gwen Redman to ask her to speak with her husband, Don, about accepting the responsibility of raising my children should God choose not to heal me. Gwen immediately began to cry. "I refuse to believe that God will not heal you."

I replied quietly to Gwen, "I understand. Really, I do, but Gwen, you have to be strong, and we have to be realistic. God could have chosen to heal me at any point along the way. We have been at this for so long now, and the longer it goes, the more I believe that he would expect me to be wise about this issue and make the best decisions possible in whatever time I have left."

My father had moved into the Daytona Beach area only a few

miles from my house a few years earlier to be closer to my son, whom he has a very special relationship with. Making this decision about my children's future was particularly difficult given my dad's relationship with my son. My father would be devastated at the news. I would have to face that music. My father is a great man. He has many wonderful qualities and loves both of my children but especially my son. We had seen a real progression in my mother's Alzheimer's over the last few months, and I felt that despite what both my son and my dad would want, asking the Redman's was the wisest choice.

This opened up another can of worms. My relationship with my father had become strained a little over the years, and I had learned to adopt a "don't ask, don't tell" policy of diplomacy around him. That limited his ability to help. He felt frustrated during this time, and most of the time, I was physically exhausted and unable to try at this juncture to resolve the situation so avoidance became my guide. The Redman's were good people, and Don was a passionate man when it comes to families.

He came by one day when I was really not feeling well at all and said, "I've spoken to both of your children, and they want to be with Papa more—especially now." Well, the circumstances between my father and I found their way into the conversation, and Don had suggested that my daughter, Cassidy, was the tool to healing this situation. He also insisted that the situation be addressed or they would not be able to help. I knew Don to be a man of his word, and I knew he wasn't just making conversation. So, slowly, we began to work on that situation, and Don was very much right. Cassidy had great techniques, for a child of eleven, at making Papa understand things Mommy wasn't quite up to. God speaks through children in marvelous ways. They are truly small wonders.

There was the trial of failing friendship. My closest friendship on earth, the one that was my vivid reminder of heaven's wonder had all but failed when I needed it the most. I made the remark to one friend that failure in my friendship with Doug was like going through a divorce all over again. This time though, it felt like I had more to lose than I did going through my marital divorce. Doug and I have been through more together than some married couples have to go through and always we have been each other's support. I had left for Gainesville with Doug being very angry with me for reasons I did not understand. It was not as if I could control being sick. This threw my world even further out of balance. I felt as though I was losing a part of my identity. I felt as though I was emotionally dying which seemed to match my physical condition.

There was the ever-present threat of unemployment. I needed desperately the insurance benefits that came with my job, but being unable to work caused a constant threat that my boss would at some point run out of patience and terminate me. Even if he did not terminate me, there was the co-worker who was trying to muscle me out of a job.

The icing on the cake of trials though was that a foreclosure action had begun on my home. My mortgage had recently been sold to another mortgage company. The former mortgage company had sent one copy of the paperwork to sale department and another copy to the foreclosure department by accident. *Wow!* I was being served with a notice of foreclosure. How does this stuff happen? I immediately got in touch (head throbbing and all) with the former mortgage company. They basically said it was out of their hands, as they had sold the mortgage, and it was my problem. I called the new mortgage company and explained the dilemma. They very kindly faxed a letter over to me saying that my mortgage was current and they had no wish to foreclose on the property. I faxed all the documentation along with a letter of what I understood to be the circumstances to both the foreclosure attorney's office and a local attorney in that same area I happened to know very well. The whole process probably took no longer than twelve hours or so. I figured that we were all reasonable people, and this could be easily resolved. Well, I was wrong. As of the writing of this book, I'm still fighting this battle, some twenty-four months later.

This is what you would call "The Long Season" of trials. It is why I chose to write this book. If you have ever felt that the weight of the world was falling down on you, I want you to know that there is someone else out there who understands that feeling. God understands that feeling too. There is no feeling that we as Christians experience that Jesus did not have to endure during his time on this earth. Each of us has our own trials that we have to walk through. What we have to remember as we walk through them is that faith is a gift. And God finishes our faith as he starts it, as a gift. One of two things will happen when you face trials, you will either move toward a pattern of self-reliance or you will desperately cry out and seek him. Growing faith often begins with what seems like chaos. You will find yourself in a situation where you have come to the end of your own means. When you cry out to God, when you seek him desperately, God does something amazing. He rewards you with more faith.

For everyone born of God overcomes the world. This is the victory that has overcome the world, even our faith.

1 John 5:3-5 (NIV)

Call upon Me in the day of trouble; I will deliver you, and you shall glorify Me.

Psalm 50: 14-16

I have told you these things, so that in me you may have peace. In this world you will have trouble. But take heart! I have overcome the world.

John 16.33 (NIV)

One way I overcame during the long season of trials was to remember. I *remembered* that Christ overcame all the evil of this world and having done so, he promises that in the end we are all victorious. I *remembered* that faith does not grow in the basement of self-entitlement. It grows most often in the field of service. I tried to find ways to serve no matter what my circumstance. I strived to be used of God, to be a witness right where I was. No matter how frail or how little you may have, there is someone somewhere who can benefit by the place God has allowed you to be in. I *remembered* all that Jesus gave up because of his love for me. He gave up heaven itself. He gave up the most perfect place anyone has ever known to come down to a sin-ridden earth to endure suffering and shame and poverty so that I might know who he is and might have the opportunity to live an eternal life with him. I *remembered* how far I have fallen and how undeserving I am and then I *remembered* his faithfulness. Remembering brings hope.

This may not change your circumstances. My thoughts are indeed not God's thoughts and I have no way of predicting the outcome of your circumstances anymore than I could have predicted my own. I can promise you though, that if you start with remembering whom God is and remembering who you are in him, then you will shift your focus off of your circumstance and how *you* will solve it and start looking for how God will resolve it. Remembering his faithfulness brings not only hope, but also peace.

Sufficient Grace

Compassionate Grace

I am moved by how compassionate God is. Most Christians are familiar with the verse that Paul wrote in 2 Corinthians 12:9, "And He said to me, "My grace is sufficient for you, for My strength is made perfect in weakness." Therefore most gladly I will rather boast in my infirmities, that the power of Christ may rest upon me." In 2 Corinthians 3:5, Paul also wrote, "Not that we are sufficient of ourselves to think of anything as being from ourselves, but our sufficiency is from God." Some key phrases in these passages include "...that the power of Christ may *rest* upon me" and "our sufficiency is from God" (Emphasis added). I don't think it is possible to walk through something so difficult as my situation, holding on to your faith and not know that God is compassionate and that his grace really is sufficient.

There are verses that speak about Jesus' compassion while he was on this earth. In Luke 7:11-17, Jesus came upon a funeral procession, and his heart was touched by the mother, a widow who had lost her only son. Luke 7:13 says, "When the Lord saw her, his heart went out to her and he said, "Don't cry."

That wasn't the last time Jesus was moved with compassion.

When Jesus went to see Mary and Martha about Lazarus... "When Jesus saw her weeping, and the Jews who had come along with her also weeping, he was deeply moved in spirit and troubled. 'Where have you laid him?' he asked. 'Come and see, Lord,' they replied. Jesus wept." (John 11:33-35, NIV). Matthew 9:36 tells us, "But when He saw the multitudes, He was moved with compassion for them, because they were weary and scattered, like sheep having no shepherd." Matthew 20:24 says, "So Jesus had compassion and touched their eyes. And immediately their eyes received sight, and they followed Him."

It was compassion itself that drove Jesus to give up the perfection of heaven and come down to this earth to endure great suffering. My fellow sufferer, nothing you or I can experience can compare to the suffering that Christ took on for you and me. He was put through a humiliating trial and was beaten beyond recognition, and after all of that, he was nailed with the equivalent of our modern day railroad ties to a cross where the greatest suffering of all took place, separation from God the Father, the ultimate suffering. My understanding of what makes hell such an awful place is not the sin that we commit or the everlasting fire but that fact that we are forever separated from God and thereby forever separated from his Grace. That is Hell.

Yes, there was grace sufficient in my suffering, and if you look, you can find grace sufficient in yours as well. I will give you some examples of God's grace and compassion in my suffering so that maybe you can identify aspects of his sufficiency and compassion in your own circumstance.

I've already mentioned the Redman's. What a Godsend these people were to me. God used them as instruments in several places throughout my circumstance. At one point Doug had suggested a book by Larry Burkette that his mother had cherished during her struggle. It was titled, *Damaged But Not Broken*.[1] It was however, out of print and despite my limited ability to get out and go places, I tried some used bookstores and even libraries. I was unable to locate a copy of the book. Gwen Redman dug up a copy on ebay of all things. Larry Burkette is well known for being the founder of Christian Financial Concepts. It is a ministry dedicated to helping Christians make the most of their financial situation. He has authored several books and had a radio show, which used to air daily. Larry's life was eventually ended on this earth by a bout with cancer. He began writing the book when he was first diagnosed with cancer in his shoulder blade and finished it not knowing what his final outcome would be. It was a powerful piece of encouragement to me, and I am saddened that it is no longer in print. I cherish every word. Larry's ministry is still going very strong and is based in Gainesville, Georgia.

I've also already mentioned to you the powerful encouragement that found its way to me through God's music, especially that written and performed by Mark Schultz. There were others whose music was also touching. If you can encourage someone who is going through a long illness or are looking for a means of doing so, offering the gift of a CD or a book may go farther than you can imagine. At my lowest times, I had these great believers to turn to. There was also my very faithful Pastor Matt Walker who allowed me to cry and vent, prayed faithfully with me, called, and visited me in the hospital. He was never too irritated or too tired of my situation to offer a word of encouragement.

My dear friend, Doug spent so many hours in the early stages of this illness trying desperately to find alternative means of helping me get well. My fondest memories though are of his prayers. Some people on this earth have the gift of prayer and Doug Williams is one of them. He can pray prayers so sweet that tears roll uncontrollably down my cheeks. My friends Belinda, Pam, and Joyce who were always on call to make sure that I had not one trip alone to the emergency room or to Shands Hospital. They were always so faithful. There was also my dad. Wow! You think when grow up, go to college, and get a good job that you are finally done depending on your parents. So much grace came through my dad. He never stopped trying to help financially, with food, trip assistance, and child-care. I owe my dad a debt I will never be able to repay. He keeps saying I don't have to, but that's the sort of debt you always want to repay. You are just not able to ever. That kind of sacrificial love is what

Jesus offered us on the cross. You can't repay it. All you can do is accept it. You can accept it and know that there is nothing you did to deserve it other than you are his child.

I was blessed with sufficient grace when the litigation started on the house to have known a diligent attorney, Holiday Hunt Russell. I had worked with him extensively on another case, and because of that, he offered to handle my battle against the mortgage company for me, understanding that I had no means of paying him. Lawyers rarely do pro-bono because if they do too much, it's hard for them make their practice thrive. Holiday was a tool of God's compassion though and he picked up this fight for me. I had no fight left. He told me not to worry about anything that he would take care of it. The attorney working on behalf of the former mortgage company had a terrible reputation as a "foreclosure mill" that treated people very badly, and Holiday assured me that it would be his pleasure to champion this fight and show this guy that you can't always get away with treating people unjustly.

My Church Benevolence Committee came to my rescue many times and kept the utilities on when I could no longer afford such. Food showed up without my having to make a request. I had the world's greatest neurologist in Dr. Benezette. This man had saved my life on more than one occasion and never gave up on getting me a shot at a normal life.

If you look at your situation and truthfully start counting your blessings, I think that you will see that God's grace is sufficient for you. You will find his compassion in many places and coming to you in many ways. There may be times in your situation when you are so low that it is all you can do to look up. Take that time to physically make a list of your blessings. It will help you to see how God is moving in your life.

Faith itself is a gift and often in order to really appreciate it, you have to move from the chaotic to the confusing to the confident. It's a path. It's a journey. The road is hard and the way is narrow. Not many will choose to go this route we are told in the Bible. This path is the only way to grow closer in our walk with God. There is a song by the group called Third Day that says, "We must go through the valley to stand upon the Mountain of God."[2] We have to be able to see our circumstances, our lives through the understanding of who God is. Whatever fruit you bear, whatever service you can offer in your circumstance is directly related to your understanding of who God is. Is how you view your present identity equal with how God is viewing your present identity? God views you as forgiven, rooted in Christ, rescued, and reconciled. Is that how you view your present identity? When you look at who you are in him, then you can see the nature of the fruit that may seem distant for you right now. You can see strength, power, patience, joy and even thankfulness.

The Hope of Glory

To them God willed to make known what are the riches of the glory of this mystery among the Gentiles: which is Christ in you, the hope of glory. ...Colossians 1:27

I knew the road of faith was a journey. I just would never have imagined only a few short years ago that I would have undergone two brain surgeries by the age of forty-one. Here I was nonetheless. I could stand, walk, and speak, and although I was hairless, I considered myself quite lucky.

I had not returned Doug's calls following the second surgery. I wasn't sure I could bear any possibility of our friendship being less than incredible at this point in my life. I was also working diligently to remain as calm and optimistic as possible. I was afraid that another argument or disappointment from Doug would dash what little remaining hope was left.

Doug continued to call me and leave messages over Memorial Day. His messages were kind and sweet and he seemed to sound concerned, but I was really apprehensive. By Wednesday, I had been home a couple of days and missing him terribly. He called and left a message that he was coming up to see me. Good move on his part. I had no choice at this point but to return his call. I was definitely not up to seeing anyone, and I certainly did not want to fight with Doug. I was very self-conscious about my appearance. (I was bald for crying out loud.) My face was hollow because I had been unable to tolerate food. I was pale. I thought to myself, *Absolutely not!* I dialed Doug's number.

He answered almost immediately. "Hey, I've been trying to reach you. How did it go?"

"I got your messages. Thank you. They were very kind. I was not permitted to use my cell phone in Intensive Care." I replied cautiously.

Doug seemed a little surprised. "You were in Intensive Care? Was there a problem?"

"No, they put me in there so they could drill a hole in my head and insert a tube to monitor the pressure."

"Wow! What was that like?" Doug asked with sincere curiosity.

"Well, Doug, I have to tell you that it was not my finest moment. Listen, I got the message you left me this morning."

"Yeah, I'm coming up on Friday. I want to visit with you a little while." Doug interjected.

"Well, I have to tell you that I don't think that is a good idea." I replied carefully.

"But you always complain that we don't get to see each other enough." Doug stuck to his guns.

"Yes, I know, but my recovery is critical right now, and I came home with a fever—not to mention that I have no hair. I don't really want you to see me this way." I tried to explain everything that had seemed so reasonable to me.

"I don't care how you look, I want to come up and see you," he insisted.

"I'll take you dinner. We'll eat sushi." Doug and I loved sushi. It was our favorite food.

"Doug, I appreciate that offer. I really do. I am just not up to this." Then he hit me with the punch.

"Annie, I want to have a chance for us to resolve the problem we ran into before you left for Gainesville."

I thought to myself, *How is that going to happen? Are you going to take back not being there for me when I was having brain surgery?* I was quiet for a moment, trying to think (which usually drove Doug nuts), and that was all the time he needed to let me know that his mind was made up and he'd see me on Friday. I had lost the argument and was completely frustrated by that.

My children had a chance to go to Disney World for the weekend with some friends. I felt that they needed such an opportunity very much and with Doug coming, I wasn't sure how things would go so I thought it best to have them out of the house. My children adored Doug and I did not want their opinions colored by anything that had happened or might happen.

Doug came up on Friday regardless of my further attempts to persuade him otherwise. We talked until the wee hours of the morning. We ate Sushi, and we went to the movies. I had a wig on most of the time, but my head would hurt sometimes so much that I had to take off the wig and put on the scarf. Doug would make jokes and try to make me comfortable. Doug had an amazing sense of humor. He treated me like royalty. We talked about how disappointed I really was at him letting me down. We had not ventured into the arena of what made him so angry at me in the first place. I knew before things really got better, we would have to go there. The purpose of his trip was to assure me that we would get past this. I wasn't so sure, and I shared that him. He left on Sunday to go home saying as he pulled out of the driveway that I would see he was right. He had said that he refused to let our friendship die after so many years. I wish I could have been as optimistic. Doug was visiting me out of a mixture of guilt and concern. I knew that unresolved guilt usually turns back into anger at some point.

Two weeks after surgery, I found myself going back to work. My boss was thrilled. He had purchased some new software in my absence and was anxious for me to get it up and running. Dr. Benezette had released me to go back to work cautioning me to give the tube time to create scar tissue that would allow it to stay in one place. We hoped this might help us avoid some of the problems we had after the first surgery. I was told that it takes anywhere from thirty to ninety days for the bottom end of the tube to create enough scar tissue to hold it in place. Prior to that, it is free to move about the peritoneal cavity. (I had undergone a surgical hysterectomy two years earlier, and I felt this gave my peritoneal cavity a little more wiggle room than the average person might have.)

I had been down for so long that I was anxious to make a good showing at work. My first week back, I was headed out back to a new production facility that was being put into operation. The walk-in doors were closed and locked, and I did not have a key to that portion of the plant so I hiked up the loading dock platform to get inside the plant. Within seconds of that move, I knew something was terribly wrong. I finished setting up the computer system and headed back to my tiny office in the server room. I was having trouble sitting and standing. Neither was very comfortable—something was wrong. I knew it was the tube. I don't know how; I just knew. I stopped in to see my immediate supervisor and let her know that I was going to have to go to the doctor's office.

Because my neurologist rarely took same day appointments, I opted to see my primary care physician. He took some vitals and sent me straight on to the ER. I got to the ER, and the doctors set out making sure that the tube was still in place. After we were certain there was no permanent damage done, and they had managed to alleviate some of the stabbing discomfort, they offered the only advice they could. "Stop climbing loading docks."

I went back to work the next day and explained to the boss that the bottom of the tube was able to move at least for a while. They offered to buy me a new chair. I thought that was really sweet. The Vice-President motioned for me to lean in close so he could say something to me privately. I did and he said, "Next time, I'll be happy to hunt you down a key." We both chuckled. I blushed a little. I had started out only working until about four in the afternoons instead of five. I just didn't quite have as much energy as I would have liked.

My dad had purchased me two wigs to help me with my vanity until my hair grew back. I looked fashionable at work, but June in Florida was sweltering; under the wig it was even worse. All that heat contributed to my fatigue. After a week of vanity, I went back to the scarves. It was just too hard to fight the heat. I still wore the wigs if we went out to dinner or I went anywhere where people did not know me. I also wore them to church. I found that at work and home though, I had to be comfortable.

Through July and August, we fought off the rejection of the tube. This meant that I had to go back on the crazy pills. I was willing to endure it though for a season if it meant that I was going to get my shot at a normal life. During this time, Dr. Benezette was always so encouraging. He assured me, "You have done so much in such a short period of time and you do nothing normal. I am confident that you will get your shot at a normal life." I held on to that hope for all it was worth.

One thing I knew by then, God had not brought me that far to drop me on my laurels. Throughout that time, I continued using all of the natural supplemental treatments that Doug and I had put together. They were soothing. The crazy pills were very hard on my system, but I managed to get through the daily grind. On one or two occasions, I had to take the medication at work to offset the stabbing pain of the tube. This proved to be a really challenging problem. At one point, another member of the staff had to drive me home because I was clearly not capable of working or driving.

By September, we had to come to terms with the fact that we were just not making enough progress with the tube. By that time, I had come to have my symptomology down to a science again. The stabbing pains would lead to fluid backing up in my head. I could lie in bed at night (on one side only; the side opposite the shunt), and the tube would shift. The only way to keep it from shifting was to lie flat. This was usually uncomfortable for me. If I leaned over too far or allowed my children to sit on my lap, the tube would shift. Once the tube would shift, it would become at least partially blocked and without fluid being able to flow out, fluid would begin to back up into my head. This would cause the pressure we had gone to all this trouble to alleviate. There were some days when I could only put in a few hours at work and some days when I could not go in at all. I still was doing 200% better than before the surgery. It just wasn't what I had envisioned. It was much harder.

It was time to get in touch with the neurosurgeon at Shands. Dr. Benezette put in a call and we were informed that Dr. Richter was leaving the staff, and they would have to assign me to a new surgeon. I was to be assigned to Dr. Wallace. I was given an appointment to meet with him. Dr. Wallace was rather young (in his 30's) and was very upwardly mobile at Shands. The staff told me that he was a brilliant surgeon. We did not really hit it off well though. He let me know early on that he had inherited this case, and it did not really look good on his record. I began to explain the troubles we had been experiencing, and he listened for only a moment when he piped in to tell me shunt patients have their tubes replaced on average of six times in the first five years. When I asked why, he said, "We never really know with Pseudo-Tumor patients. The symptoms reoccur without explanation, and we wind up replacing the tube just to satisfy the symptomology."

My eyebrows still furrow at the thought of this explanation. I told Dr. Wallace, "I did not sign up for any such thing. I am trying everything possible to get to obtain a normal life."

Dr. Wallace said, "There is absolutely no chance of that happening." He told me, "This is as good as you are going to get." At that point, I began to cry. I told him angrily something was wrong with the tube and it needed to be fixed. He said, "I will schedule some tests. Someone will be in touch." With that, he walked out leaving me in tears.

I came back and met with Dr. Benezette. I begged him, "Please find a way to fix this so that I do not have to go back and see Dr. Wallace again. I cannot take the discouragement!" Dr. Benezette assured me that Dr. Wallace was just plain wrong.

He told me, "Dr. Wallace obviously had not read the file carefully or he would know that you do not do anything normal." He also said, "There is absolutely no reason for you to have to have six shunt replacements." He said that he believed that God would give me the chance to overcome this. "I would really like to have those test results, Annie, but I'll understand if you don't want to go back to Shands and take them." Boy, Dr. Benezette was good. I had to learn not to underestimate him in the future. I agreed to the tests.

My friend, Joyce went with me for the first round of tests. I had been told that I would be having an x-ray and CT scan. I asked if the CT scan required having the ingested dye. I was told it would. I explained that I had a very difficult time tolerating that dye and we may need to plan on a different test. I was told that the technicians in the CT department would be advised and be ready to help. I was nervous when I arrived. The orders were wrong. There was a mix-up and the sign-in nurse saw it right away. This delayed the testing. It seemed like an hour before all of that was straightened out. I had an early afternoon appointment with Dr. Wallace and so far we were not on schedule. The technician brought out a bottle of blue Gatorade. University of Florida, home of the Gators is where Gatorade was developed (hence the name). On top of the bottle was a plastic cup. The technician began to explain to me about the intervals of ingesting the dye that was mixed with the Gatorade. My eyes kind of glazed over, and he stopped talking and asked if I was okay. I explained that I had let them know that I didn't tolerate the dye well when I made the appointment and then despite my efforts to refrain, a tear slipped down my cheek. The technician asked me to wait and he left the waiting area.

Next out came the nurse who I had been introduced to during the first surgery. She remembered me, and I remembered her. She was very kind and wanted to reassure me that all I had to do was try. She said, "If at any time, the liquid substance becomes intolerable, you could inform the sign-in nurse. We will come and get you and take you back and inject the dye via your arm." She was a wonderful nurse with a very calming bedside manner. I began attempting to get the dye down. Joyce had brought a book but managed to make conversation to keep things light-hearted while I was undertaking my difficult task. After about thirty minutes of trying to ingest the dye, I was becoming very nauseated. This was a feeling I had learned to hate. The constant pain in my head made me nauseated all the time. (Since I was a small child, I had a real fear of throwing up. I had a very difficult time tolerating nausea.) Joyce informed the sign-in nurse that I was having difficulty. One look at my now greenish face confirmed that.

The very sweet nurse returned and took me back to a room full of Lazy-Boy recliners. She picked one out for me and told me to sit down. She then started an IV so that she could get the dye injected. Once enough dye was in, then I would be taken back to the CT machine for the scan. It would take about fifteen minutes for the dye to be completely drained out of the bag into my arm. By this time, we were seriously behind schedule, and I was worried that Dr. Wallace would not see me. I explained this to the nurse who said she would have someone call upstairs to neurosurgery and let them know I'd be late.

While sitting and waiting, I was reading Dr. Yancey's Book, *Where is God When It Hurts*. A lady sitting in a chair next to me asked, "What's the answer to the question?"

I questioned her, "Pardon me?" She repeated the question and then pointed to the book. I told her, that "I am only a few chapters into the book and as of yet do not have all the answers but I have some." I took this as an opportunity to serve. It was a chance to make something positive out of a really bad situation for me. We began to carry on a conversation about how God authored pain and how it acts as a warning system. That led her to ask me if I was a believer. I answered, "My faith is all that gets me through some days." She said she was a believer as well and that she was there assisting a family member. Now being Compadres of sorts, I asked about the family member's illness, and she asked about mine. I assured her that there are times when I felt pretty down, but I never felt as though God didn't care. "I want to reassure you that God is present in your situation as well." By the time the conversation was ending, my IV was done dripping and we had prayed together. As we parted ways, she indicated that she hoped I found the answer to the question. I told her, "The point to is to keep seeking it." She smiled.

As soon as the test was complete, I asked for directions to the restroom, where I promptly threw up all of the dye. I got cleaned up, and Joyce and I headed upstairs. I had ample time on the ride over to Shands to prep Joyce for Dr. Wallace. Once we got to neurosurgery, she decided she would wait in the waiting area. I didn't blame her one bit. I went in for my appointment, and Dr. Wallace informed me that the CT scan and the x-ray were both normal.

I asked, "What does that mean?" He repeated the results. I asked him in frustration "Does either one of those test show whether or not fluid is flowing through the tube or if the tube is somehow blocked?"

Dr. Wallace lost his patience and said rather indignantly, "No, they do not!"

I got upset and asked, "Why on earth would you put me through the test then?"

He answered, "Because I needed to make sure that the tube was not dislodged."

I pointed out in frustration, "No one had suggested that the tube was dislodged."

He said, "I have no intention of operating on you unnecessarily."

I replied insistently, "I have no intentions of allowing you to do three times what has already not been successful two other times." I also told him, "You would not live like this or make your wife live like this when you had the power to do something about it." (I had noticed a wedding band on his finger.) I hit the pitch home. "But you are forcing me to live like this!" He said he would order more tests and curtly left the room. I was once again in tears of frustration. I walked out, and when Joyce asked how it went, I told her not well and we were leaving.

Once again, I met with Dr. Benezette. I begged him, "Please find a way to fix this without making me go back to see Dr. Wallace again." I told Dr. Benezette, "You have always managed to pull a rabbit out of a hat every time I needed you to before."

Dr. Benezette gently reminded me "I am not a surgeon, Annie." He also said, "But I won't make you go back anymore if you do not want to. I understand completely. It would be a shame to come this far and not get the right tests after all this." (Boy, he's really good!) Within a few more seconds he had me agreeing to go back for the additional tests. A week or so later two more tests were scheduled. I was set for an MRI and nuclear medicine study. A nuclear medicine study involves more dye. This time, though it would be injected directly into my shunt via the port in my head. I would not have to drink it. This meant that they would have to shave a portion of my head, which had just now begun to have enough hair to cover the scars. The MRI would be conducted to make sure that no tumors had formed along the spine during the time we had been fighting this illness. An MRI could be dangerous as it shuts down a programmable shunt. However, since we knew the shunt was already malfunctioning, I assumed the test to be worth the risk. Following the test, the shunt would have to be reprogrammed to be opened again so that fluid could flow through it. Following that procedure, an x-ray needed to be obtained to verify the shunt opening.

Joyce being a real trooper, made the trip up with me again. We met with the sign-in nurse who sent me to the nuclear medicine lab. It was very cold there. Shortly thereafter, a nurse came in and introduced herself. She said, "I will be assisting a neurosurgical medical student who will be performing the test." I also met a technician who would be monitoring the results of the scan. The nurse took my vitals and then paged the student. He came in. He was a very nice and very tall young man who looked like he was about seventeen. I made some jokes about just having gotten hair, and he was sensitive enough to pick right up on it.

He asked, "Would you like me to try to inject the dye without having to shave your head?"

I asked in shock, "Can you really do that?"

He said, "the port sticks out pretty well, and if you are willing to be uncomfortable for a minute or two, I think I could do it."

Uncomfortable had become my middle name. I was so excited at the possibility of keeping my hair that I barely noticed the pain of the large needle that was injected into my brain. Within just a few seconds he let me know "I've got all the dye in, and my portion of the test is over with. I am going to leave you in the hands of the technicians who will complete the test."

The technician started the scan explaining to me. "We are watching fluid flow through the tube." I must admit that the technology fascinated me. As the fluid moved about halfway down my chest it suddenly stopped. The technician said, "Hmmm, that's odd!" He came up and pushed on the spot where the dark line had stopped and there was squirt of dark fluid that shot out at a ninety-degree angle. Once again, the technician said, "Hmmm!" He pushed again on the same spot with the same results. He did that once or twice more before I made the comment that I was not the Pillsbury Dough Boy. He then asked me to get up and walk around for a few minutes and then come back. I did as instructed. He started the scan again with exactly the same results. He tried pushing a few centimeters below the original spot and fluid again shot out at a ninety-degree angle.

I asked, "Is there a problem?"

He indicated, "No, I am just not used to seeing such results." He said, "You will need to go over to another building for the MRI." I did as instructed. Dr. Wallace was not to have time to meet with me that day. I would have to make another trip back in a few days to go over the results.

Joyce and I came back the first week of October, a few days after the tests to meet with Dr. Wallace. He walked in and said very soberly, "The nuclear medicine study concluded that the shunt has defects."

I asked, "What kind of defects?"

He said, "It appears to be leaking."

I asked, "Where?"

He indicated in his short manner, "It appears to be leaking in more than one place. In fact, it appears to have several leaks throughout the length of the tube, and there is no sign that fluid is ever reaching the bottom of the tube."

Dr. Wallace did not apologize or pat me on the back for being right. Instead, he stated flatly, "I am scheduling surgery for Thursday morning, but you will be in a waiting position as you were during the last scheduled surgery."

I was shocked. "But today is Monday."

He said rather curtly, "It is Thursday or not at all." I agreed to be back on Thursday. Joyce and I rode home without much conversation. What could be said? I was heading in for brain surgery number three in less than six months. It was unimaginable. Yet, it was happening. This was not at all what I had hoped for. I had gone over to Shands with the Hope of Glory. I was hoping that God would have a simple fix to my problems. You could have knocked me over at this point. I was worried about coming home to tell my children and my family. My son had begged me not to go back to Shands. He said he knew that they would find something terrible. He had thrown himself on the bed in tears when I announced that Joyce and I would be going on Monday for the tests. How do you comfort an eight-year-old boy who has watched his mother go through so much? The conversation with Justin Elijah would be the one I would dread the most.

Strength Only From God

The LORD is my rock and my fortress and my deliverer; My God, my strength, in whom I will trust; My shield and the horn of my salvation, my stronghold.

Psalms 18:2

It is God who arms me with strength, and makes my way perfect.

Psalms 18:32

I let the words sink in over and over in my mind on the ride home from Shands. I honestly did not know from where I would get the strength to endure this latest development. I began to break the picture down into smaller pieces that were easier to deal with.

First things first, I'd have to talk to my children. Justin and Cassidy would have to be reassured that things were as God had ordained them to be. I also would have to make arrangements for them to stay with someone.

Then I would have to call Pastor Matt and let him know.

I would also have to call Dr. Benezette's office.

I would have to inform work. This would probably wind up my job for sure. I couldn't worry about that now though.

I had to call several family members and my ex-husband. There wasn't much time.

I first spoke with my Children, Justin and Cassidy. Justin immediately broke down saying, "I told you this would happen!"

Cassidy had a tear rolling down her cheek but told Justin, "It will be okay. Mommy has to go." I held them both as close as I could and assured them that God will be with us no matter

what happens. "We can pray and ask God to make this easier for both of you." I tried to reassure them that this new surgeon while I didn't like his bedside manner had a reputation as a brilliant surgeon and was considered to be one of the best on staff at Shands. They slept with me that night, and although I knew I would not be able to sleep with them in the bed, I gladly agreed to the arrangement. I needed to be close to them as much as they needed to be close to me.

I called my brother, Tony, and asked him if he would come up for the surgery. "Tammarie needs a break from having to go. The hospital environment is really hard for her after Paul's death."

"Yes, I'll go with you. I'll come up on Wednesday. I'll have to let work know." I called my dad and gave him the news. I also told him that I had asked Tony to go with me to the surgery. I spoke with Dad about bringing the kids over to Shands following the surgery. I called Selina and told her the unbelievable news. I also called Doug. He seemed frustrated.

"Why can't they get things right, Annie? What is wrong with those people?"

"I don't really know the answers to those questions, Doug, and I am real tired right now," I replied.

"I'll be praying for you, Annie."

"Thanks, Doug. That would be really good," I said as I ended the conversation. I notified work the following morning. I was going to be leaving Wednesday and heading up. My brother and I had decided to get a room nearby because we had to be at the hospital very early Thursday morning. It didn't make much sense to wear myself out not getting any sleep the night before surgery and getting up at four in the morning to drive over to Gainesville.

Tony and I had time to talk about a few things and especially my arrangements for the kids. "Things will go well. Don't worry." He tried to reassure me.

I told him, "Oddly enough, I'm not really worried." Mostly, at that point, I was just numb. Pastor Dennis Kiggins had called to say that the church would be praying for me. The hotel Tony and I picked out to stay at had an afternoon snack buffet around four o'clock. We had finished up all the pre-surgery testing, but we just wanted to get something light. We both were in the mood for Wendy's. We found one down the road just a little way from the hotel. We grabbed a quick bite and headed back. I told Tony, "I am kind of tired out, and my head hurts. I am going to call it an early night." Tony was in the room next to mine. I showered, prayed, and sank into a Max Lucado book. I needed Max's encouragement this night.

A few minutes into the book, Doug called. "I just wanted to let you know that I'll be praying for you tonight and in the morning." Things between he and I were still quite strained, and I was very glad and surprised a little to get the call.

"I will try and call you tomorrow before the surgery if there is time, Doug."

"Okay, well do you want me to pray with you?" he asked nervously.

"I guess you could do that if you want to." I thanked him after the prayer and hung up. I finished the chapter I was reading and drifted off to sleep.

I awoke early the next morning and snuck downstairs for a cup of coffee, which was complimentary. I wasn't supposed to eat or drink anything but I had a pretty good idea that I'd be waiting awhile based on my experience, and I needed the comfort of my morning coffee. To my surprise, my brother was already downstairs and questioned me about the coffee. "I thought you weren't supposed to eat or drink anything?"

I told him "It will be hours before they operate. It will be okay." So we sat together while he ate, and I had my coffee. Then we checked me out of the hotel and put my stuff in Tony's truck and headed to the hospital. We had been waiting about two hours or so when to my surprise, my dad, mom and children showed up. I was thrilled to see them, but I had not expected them until after the surgery. We waited for a few more hours before they called me up to pre-op. Tony and I headed up to pre-op where he was delighted to see a plasma television on a small swinging arm in my pre-op area. He was immediately engrossed. The nurse came by and started the IV. She made light conversation. The anesthesiologist came in and made the usual introductions. Next in was a familiar medical student whom I had met during my last stay.

He assured me, "Dr. Wallace is a great surgeon, and the students on this case are very excited to be working with him." He said, "Well, you know this procedure; do you have any questions?"

I indicated, "No, but I'd like to ask you to give me a new scar abdominally."

He said, "That is not likely. Dr. Wallace will not agree to that."

I asked "Why?"

He explained, "We are brain surgeons and not abdominal or general surgeons, and we do not like to mess around in the abdominal area."

I pleaded, "The existing scar has been opened twice already and is getting more difficult to heal each time."

He said, "I understand that, but I am confident that Dr. Wallace will not agree to this change." At this point, Tony piped in and said, "She said she wants a new scar!" He said it deliberately and in a quiet yet booming voice. (Did I mention that Tony is a football coach that is over 6 feet tall and a very well built guy with a deep voice?) The small built med student immediately assured us both that he would see to it. He then made a very quick exit from the room. Tony went back to watching the plasma screen. I giggled. Within a few minutes, the nurse was back to take me away. Tony assured me once again that things would be fine. Within a few moments after that, I was off to sleep once more.

I awoke some time later to find it was nighttime and that Tony was calling my name. "Annie, you still have hair."

I said "really?"

Tony replied, "Give me your hand. You can feel it." I was shocked to find that I was only missing small patches of hair. I peeked under the covers. Before I could see anything, Tony said, "Oh yeah, you got a new scar, too." I smiled. I drifted off a little.

Next thing I knew, my two precious children were in the room along with my parents. Dad asked, "How do you feel?"

I answered with a smile, "I feel so much better that I can't believe it." They left shortly thereafter to head to the hotel where they were all staying for the night. I went back to sleep.

I awoke a few hours later around midnight realizing that my head no longer hurt and that the shunt felt much tighter in my head. I could also feel for the first time the shunt tube in my neck and in my chest and abdomen. It was an odd sensation. I could feel it all the way down. I got up and went for a walk. The tube was draining well. I knew this because I needed to make several trips to the bathroom throughout the night.

The next morning a medical student came in to say, "Dr. Wallace left town for the weekend immediately following the surgery, but he wanted you to know that all went very well." He asked, "Is it true that you have been up several times during the night?" I said that it was expecting a lecture. He asked, "How do you feel?"

"I am amazed that my head does not have any pressure."

"The tubing had holes throughout its entire length. This new shunt should function much better." He asked, "Would you like to go home?" I looked at him in utter disbelief.

"Absolutely!"

He said, "Well you can. You're already up and around, and I don't see any reason to keep you." I asked about follow up appointments. He said that Dr. Wallace told me not to come back unless I had a problem. He would not get an argument out of me on that one. I called my family to pick me up, and we headed home. Tony stayed one more night with us in Daytona and then headed back to South Florida where he lived.

A week later, I was in Dr. Benezette's office getting stitches and staples out. I could not believe the difference. Dr. Benezette had started me on the Lyrica immediately following surgery, and within two weeks, I was off that medication altogether. There was no rejection this time. *What a blessing that was all by itself!*

I had arrived home to find that my job had finally been given to the pushy co-worker. I vowed not to worry about it. God had been faithful through so much. I did not know how, but he would be faithful through this too. The next day, I got a telephone call from my boss asking me to come back to work. I told him that I thought my co-worker had been given my job. He said he had made that change but it had not worked out. I told him I could be there if he needed me. When I arrived, I found out that the pushy co-worker had a breakdown of sorts and was let go the first day she took over my position.

I was still tired but very glad to be going back to work. I loved my work although the environment was difficult. I was able to start doing things with my kids very slowly. It was so good to have them home with me all the time. I was still going to bed very early every evening, but I was okay with that. My children and I do not miss any opportunity to say I love you. We know that those moments are precious.

I did very well with this shunt all things considered. I still was not 100%, but I was 200% better than I had been during the last eighteen months. I kept smiling all the time. People at Church kept commenting on my smile, and I would say that I felt like I had been given my life back. I had not relied on any strength of my own. I had nothing to rely on. God had provided me strength, friends, family, a great neurologist, and many more blessings to endure this long trial. I had so much to be thankful for. For the first time in many months, I was past the apprehension of immediate impending death. All of us will die at some point unless we happen to be among the few who are still alive when the Lord returns. I don't fear death itself. As a matter of fact, it will be relief for me. Someday it will be peace for me. However, I was very glad to be still here to work for God and to be a mother to my children.

About a month or so after my surgery, my son was playing

with the next-door neighbor when he rather flatly complained of a stomachache. It did not stop him from playing but later that evening as he prepared for bed, he mentioned it again. "Mom, my stomach still hurts."

"Has it been hurting this whole time?" I asked curiously.

"Yes Ma'am" he replied.

"Hmmm. Well, take a warm bath and I'll see what I have for that," I said soothingly. After his bath, Justin immediately went to bed and was quickly sound asleep. I can tell that every mother reading this story is already questioning the symptomology. When eight-year-old boys go to bed voluntarily and early to boot, we moms know that something is amiss.

The next morning I awoke to find Justin sleeping next to me. He woke up with a sense of urgency. "Mommy, I think I have to throw up."

I sat straight up. "Justin, go to the bathroom, hurry." Sure enough he began throwing up. I quickly deduced he had a pretty good fever cooking. I woke up Cassidy and let her know that I needed to take Justin to the emergency room. She was concerned but very understanding. I called the next-door neighbors to stay with Cassidy until someone arrived.

The nurses in the emergency room were stunned to find out that I was there for someone other than myself. They treated my son with great kindness. A CT scan was ordered, and the doctor on duty let me know that he was pretty sure that my son had appendicitis. Justin flipped out at the suggestion and began to insistently cry, "Mommy, I don't want an operation."

I realized that his fear was based mostly on my experience. I did my best to assure him that everything would be okay. "Justin, lots of people have their appendix out. Remember that Angel had hers out not long ago. This is not like Mommy's surgeries. This is a really simple procedure."

By the time, the CT test was ready, Papa and Grandma had shown up, and my ex-husband was on the way. He had picked up

Cassidy and dropped her off at his parents' house. In the meantime, the CT test confirmed appendicitis. A surgeon was called in and introduced to our family. Justin was very sleepy because they had given him pain relief medication. My dad and ex-husband, John, had stepped out to the lobby. I was left in the exam room with Grandma who kept asking what was going on. The surgeon explained, "I am a guest surgeon here visiting. You do not have to use my services, but I am offering them. I practice down near Titusville, but I heard about your son and offered to perform the surgery."

"That is very kind of you. My son is very nervous, I've recently undergone my third brain surgery, and he is naturally afraid of the word *surgery*," I explained.

"Do you mind if I ask about your condition?" the surgeon asked politely.

"Not at all. I have a condition called Pseudo-Tumor Cerebrai. I've had three brain surgeries in the last twelve months. This has been very hard on my children so you can understand my son's apprehension."

"You have more than one child?" the surgeon quickly deduced.

"Yes, I also have a daughter who is twelve." I replied. About that time, my cell phone rang as Cassidy was calling in to check on her brother. I quickly brought her up to speed and then let her know that I needed to finish my conversation with the surgeon. I told her that I would call her back shortly. "That was my daughter, Cassidy. She is worried about her little brother," I said smiling.

"I understand. We'll be operating in about thirty minutes or so as soon as we can secure an operating room."

"That quick, huh?" I was rather surprised.

"Yes, I'll call down as soon as we are ready." With that, the surgeon disappeared. I felt very peaceful about this surgeon. He had a kindness about him. A few moments later, he reappeared to let me know that it would be about two more hours before he could operate because another emergency had gone in while he was down consulting with us. He expressed a concern. "We can attempt the procedure laproscopically as long as the appendix has not ruptured. I am concerned that we might not get in there before it ruptures considering he was complaining of the pain all day yesterday and now we're having to wait two more hours. I'll do everything I can to try and perform the surgery laproscopically."

"Thank you. I've explained to Justin about laparoscopic surgery, and I know that he'd be more comfortable with that procedure. This whole thing is a little scary for him after watching me go through all I have been through." The doctor indicated that he understood completely.

After a couple of hours, Justin was taken up to the pre-op area where we met the anesthesiologist. It turned out to be the same anesthesiologist that had performed my spinal blood patch. She immediately recognized me and said, "I knew the patient's name rang a bell. How are you doing?"

"I am much better thank you. I've just had my third brain surgery, but I am doing much better." I introduced her to my son, and he had a big smile when I explained to him who she was. She promised to take good care of him, and he had no anxiety about going with her at all. I was so relieved. We were all directed to a surgical waiting area.

Shortly after arriving in the surgical waiting area, a volunteer from the hospital called my name and directed me to come to the phone at her desk. I answered the phone. "Miss Hickey, this is the anesthesiologist. I wanted to let you know that your son went under anesthesia a few moments ago without any distress. He was smiling and laughing when he fell asleep. We'll be speaking with you again following the procedure. I just didn't want you to worry." (I cannot tell you how that phone call touched my heart.)

After the surgery, the surgeon came down to let us know that Justin would have to remain overnight. "The appendix started to rupture just as I made the first laparoscopic incision. I was able to get all the fluid but I'm going to need to keep him to be absolutely sure. That fluid could make him really sick."

"I understand. I'll need to be in the room with him," I replied.

We were then directed to the recovery room area where we were allowed to see Justin.

"Mommy, it didn't hurt at all." Two seconds later, Justin was snoring. The nurse let us know that he was still pretty groggy.

Later that night when Justin was in a regular room and the family had all gone home, the surgeon came by to see us. Justin was sleeping. "I wanted to stop by and see how my little patient was doing. I'm also going to give you my cell phone number in case you have any concerns whatsoever. Feel free to call me with anything." I was a little caught off guard by this generosity.

"Do you hand out your cell phone number to all your patients?" I asked curiously.

"No, but your family has really touched my heart. You all have an amazing quality."

Without thinking I replied, "Well, we've been through a lot together."

Equally as fast the surgeon replied, "That is not it. I meet people almost everyday that have been through traumatic events. It is part of being a surgeon. You're family has something more." I paused for a moment realizing that he was right.

"You are right. It is not what we have been through. It is our faith. We believe that God directs our life and that he does not make mistakes. We believe that while living in this world brings with it trouble sometimes, God ordains all that happens in our lives and is involved in even the little things. We also believe that God perfectly planned for us three to be a family and as such we each bring gifts to this family that allow us to support each other through everything. We rely on that. Because of that, we have a very strong connection."

The surgeon contemplated my words and replied, "Yes, that is what I see in your family. I'm going to go and let you get some rest. Call me if you need anything at all."

"Thank you for everything. I feel very blessed that you were here to help with this situation," I said in gratitude to the doctor as he was leaving.

There are times in each life I believe that God orchestrates events in such a way that we know with great certainty that he is the only source of our survival. He has unusual ways of slowing us down when our lives get to busy. He draws us closer to him through trials and complications. There is no sweeter fellowship that we ever experience than that of complete dependence on God. The word *savior* takes on a completely new meaning during those times.

I Can Do Better Than That

I have, throughout this crisis, been moved by contemporary Christian music. I have made comments throughout the book about my love for this kind of encouragement. Mark Schultz is my favorite contemporary Christian artist because he writes and performs music that covers some very tough areas of life and reminds us that God is right where we are. He tells the story on his DVD, *A Night Of Stories And Songs*, that he wanted to become a singer in Nashville and how he left home in Kansas headed toward that dream. He tells about how he finally got to that goal by being divinely guided down roads he would never have chosen for himself. He also tells how going down those roads helped him to have the material necessary to write the songs he has written. He said that when he prayed and asked God to help him realize his dream because he had gotten himself in over his head that he felt God's reply was, "I can do better than that!" [1]

I love that story because it is so true. We would never choose for ourselves the paths we are guided down when we relinquish control to God. I would never have volunteered for three brain surgeries even if doing so meant great things would result. I'd have chickened out for sure. God has permitted me to walk through trials that I am still surprised at so that I will have the courage, faith and the ability to face the things that are yet to come and so that I can touch lives in a way that no ordinary circumstance would.

Since my last surgery, we have faced lots of issues that we did not anticipate. Some of those issues arose simply out of the fact that we were dealing with fairly new technology. My shunt is programmable. This is scientifically great stuff because it affords surgeon's the ability to control the shunt without surgical intervention. As with all new technology though, we learn as we go. I had been told prior to leaving shands that I should avoid those scanners at airports and that MRI machines would shut down the shunt. I was also told that I should avoid extreme heat or cold. I would have to give up my beloved tanning sessions and no snow-skiing. I was also told to avoid contact sports. *Darn*! I'd never get that NFL draft for the Dallas Cowboys I had always wanted! Beyond that, I was not given much advice. I learned the hard way that this was because know one knew what advice to give.

I had gone back to work at my old job but found that we ran into problems with heat. Manufacturing stone is primarily an unairconditioned environment in Florida. We also found that food was now a problem. I mentioned that I could now feel the tube as it ran it's entire length. I had not been able to do that previously. This new sensativity created all sorts of problems. While we had successfully managed to avoid rejection this time around, the tube still had too much maneuverability within my peritoneal cavity. This could cause periodic stabbings. Now that fluid was flowing so well, there was much for my tissues to aborb, and this created problems with nausea. The portion of the tube that runs through my chest causes a disruption in normal acids. We found that a prescription antacid was required to help normalize this. Foods that had been common for me prior to surgery were no longer acceptable. I could no longer tolerate eggs, tomatoes, most fried foods, or heavy foods. Lighter foods such as yogurt or vitamin shakes became my friends.

My boss came to see me a few days before Thanksgiving. We met at a small granite conference table outside of my office. He and the Vice President came in to tell me that I was no longer employed. I asked, "Why?" It made no sense to have waited all this time for me to get better and to let me go six or seven weeks after my return. My boss refused to give me an explanation. I was shocked and asked permission to relate the news to my staff. He agreed, which really surprised me. So I called in the other members of my team and gave them the news. The Vice-President helped me pack my things, and I left. I drove home in stunned silence.

I was met with an email shortly after arriving home from our Network Administrator. He was outsourced and as such not working at the plant. He was shocked because he had been contacted and told to terminate my connections to the network. He and I talked, and he assured me that he would do whatever he could to help me find new employment. "I am not at all happy with the way things have been handled, being let go so close to the holiday, but I hope this will give way to an even better job."

I told him, "Actually, I am sort of relieved." I applied for unemployment, Cobra'd my insurance and started looking for a new job. This I knew...God had handled all of my previous problems. This one would not be too much for him.

I met with one of the Church Elder's over finance during the time following the third surgery. I needed help with organizing my medical debt. I had insurance but not great insurance, and my medical bills had come to almost $200,000. My portion of that debt came to about $80,000. I had managed to cover some of it while I was sick but not all of it. Not working most of the time, I was amazed that any of it got covered. Now that I had gone back to work, I felt that I could face the fears my of my very bleak financial situation. Blake Thomas was incredibly encouraging and uplifting. He was also very knowledgeable about matters of finance. I immediately felt comfortable talking with Blake and had no qualms about sharing my financial circumstance. Blake was able to suggest several options for me that I had not even thought of. I had previously worked for a number of years in a position that allowed me to allocate significant funds to a couple of separate retirement funds. Blake suggested that we liquidate these funds to alleviate my concern about the debt and help me sustain some of the impact that had been created during my long absence from work. I would not have even thought of these things had I avoided meeting with Blake. He also counseled me on how best to communicate with those whose medical debt was not going to be paid off immediately.

Now that I was being laid off, I went for a second meeting with Blake. I knew that while he might not know of anyone looking to hire someone of my talents, he would have some encouragement to offer and frankly that was of equal importance to me as a job offer would have been. Blake had become a valuable resource for me because of his encouragement and his prayerful consideration of matters. He said that he would be praying that an even better job would come along and he helped me plan a spending strategy.

I was invited over to the Redman's for Thanksgiving dinner. I had at first declined the offer but then later accepted after being asked a second time. My children were spending Thanksgiving with their father and his family. I felt that it would be better to go over to Gwen and Don's than to sit at home missing my children terribly. Gwen called and asked, "Will you bring a copy of your resume?" I was surprised but agreed. I assumed she knew someone who might be looking to hire. After a wonderful dinner, I had an opportunity to speak to Gwen about the resume. She began to talk about Don's company, her position within that company, and how she was looking to change positions. Now, I like to joke that they touched something in my brain that they shouldn't have during that last surgery because sometimes I am not as quick as I used to be and sometimes just don't remember things. I totally missed the point of Gwen's conversation. A few days later, Angel, Gwen's daughter was doing a presentation for Mary Kay at a nearby restaurant and I had been invited to go. I had gotten a call from Don asking if I had plans to attend. I answered affirmatively, and he asked if he could speak with me there. I told him that would be great. After the main presentation, Don asked me to join him in a separate part of the restaurant. I did. He proceeded to talk to me about his company, and Gwen's position in it, her present desires to pursue other things. I know you're way ahead of me here, but I did not see what was coming next. Don asked, "Would you be interested in working for me?"

I answered with a stunned response, "Doing what?"

He chuckled and indicated, "You'd be managing the operations and heading up the financial and technology areas."

I told him, "Don, let me pray about this and get back to you. It sounds fantastic, and I'm not using that as ploy or anything. I have just found after everything I've been through, God's opinions come before my own." The Redmans were long-time close friends of mine, and I did not want my wanting a job to damage that friendship in any way. This was on a Saturday.

On Monday, Don called and asked, "Have you had time to pray about it yet?"

I told him that I had and that I would take the position. My children were thrilled about this development. They had come to love Mr. Don, and they had been to his office many times during my illness so they knew they would always be welcomed there. We worked out an arrangement that would allow me to work part-time through the holidays so that I could do two things: I needed to spend some quality time with my kids while they were out of school for the holiday season and I needed to wrap up some work for Doug on a legal case that I had been managing for him for the last couple of years. I had anticipated some court time coming up and needed to be available to administer those affairs. We agreed that I would come on full time at the first of the New Year.

It was a busy holiday season for us as this was the first time I had gotten to visit any of my family in well over a year. I had previously always been too sick to travel, so we had really enjoyed being able to get together for the Christmas Holiday. Being home in time for Christmas Eve service at Christ Community Church was also a very special time for us. Remembering where we had been just one year earlier gave us so much to feel blessed about during this sacred time of year. Our church had a candle-light service that was just beautiful. It was a very special time that I would not soon forget.

The only disappointment during that time was that my friendship with Doug was not showing any sign of improvement. I was still dealing with so much anger and frustration from him. I was in turn starting to get really angry at these circumstances and despite my heart's desire to just forgive everything and overlook all of his actions, I found myself trying to be persuasive in my arguments and eventually just getting frustrated. I was very angry because I felt that Doug had not been there when I needed him most. He had not been there for the second and third surgeries. After the plunge our friendship had taken right before the second surgery, I did not bother to ask him to come up for the third. When two people are angry, it is very difficult to get anything of significance accomplished. Doug hated to argue more than anything. We had gotten to the point that we rarely ended a telephone conversation with good-bye. It usually ended by one or the other of us hanging up on the other. All we did was argue these days.

A few days before Christmas, we had a huge blow-up. It was the fight of all fights. I withdrew from his legal case. I had poured more than three years of my life into this litigation all to help a friend who was not good with legalities. This case dominted my time so often. It took time away from my children. It interefered with my work. My desire was to help but it seemed as though with all of the anger, I was being blamed for everything that wasn't perfect. The pressure suddenly overwhelmed me and I snapped. I told Doug that our friendship was over. The words came out before I could stop them. I couldn't take the fighting anymore. I notified the lawyers and other professionals handling the case via email. And while I would not allow this to diminish in any way my worship on Christmas Eve, on Christmas Day, my heart was breaking.

Doug and I had over the years created a tradition I had come to cherish, of calling each other on holidays and special occasions and reserving just a small amount of time to wish each other blessings. I had no hopes that Doug would call this Christmas, but it did not make the day go by any faster. My kids traditionally spend most of

Christmas Day with their father. This year would be no different. The day dragged on at an agonizingly *slow* pace. No call came. Sometimes, like in ICU at Shands or at home by yourself on Christmas, silence, although it bears no sound, can be booming. The large chasm that had been created by our last argument seemed to loom over every part of the day.

Around lunchtime, I had begun to develop some serious stabbing pains from the tube and by four thirty, I could not tolerate the pain any longer. I was off to the emergency room with my friend Joyce in tow. Five hours later, we ascertained the obvious...the tube was stabbing me. All they could do was make me comfortable, CT the tube and make sure it was still there, and send me home. Well, this day would not go down as my most beloved Christmas memory, but I came home still saying that I was greatful for being much further along than I had been last year at this same time. I was greatful that there was a functioning tube in place—even if it was constantly letting me know that it was there.

The next morning found me tired but feeling much better. Emergency room trips had a way of wiping out all of my energy, but this one had seemed to do so more than most of my experience. I slept most of the next day. The week between Christmas and New Year's Day came and went with no word from Doug. Each day was painfully long. While I was not surprised, I was really heartbroken. I kept telling myself that some friendships have a life span and perhaps ours had reached its limits. Nevermind the fact that we had been friends for nearly forty-two years at that point—that might be as long as we were able to sustain it. That idea just seemed then and still does to me to be so very sad. I firmly believed that God put this man in my life and me in his.

I spent a lot of time praying over the holidays about the fact that I needed God to do what I could not which was to fix this friendship. I started out by asking him to change me. Change my heart so that my desires did not come above what God wanted and had planned for this friendship. I also acknowledged that God was the author of this friendship and I was not. Then I wrote Doug a letter outlining my same desires and asking him to please put away this anger and to try and remember our friendship. My next move was to ask for wise counsel from people who understood this kind of thing more than me and then wait to see what God would do.

I had new challenges all the way through the month of January. I had full time work at my new job. I had the challenges of Doug's litigation and of it getting close to the trial stage after nearly three years. I had almost immediately renounced my decision to withdraw from the case. I knew if our friendship had any chance of survival that I would have to follow through with my promises to help with the litigation. I also had the challenge of trying to cope with a new tube that was presenting physical problems all its own.

My Birthday came toward the end of January, and my kids and I felt this was a very big birthday. Normally, on my birthday, I would get a huge bouquet of flowers and an incredible phone call from Doug and all sorts of homemade accolades from my children. This year, I knew there would most likely be no flowers from Doug, but I knew that this needed to be a big birthday anyway for the sake of my kids. This was important stuff to them. Mom had survived the unthinkable and was celebrating something they were not sure they'd ever get to celebrate again. So we planned a dinner out, my ex-husband took the kids shopping for Mommy's gifts (real ones this year, not homemade), and we talked it up to everyone giving God the glory for bringing us through everything. This had to be a special day. This should have been a great day in my friendship with Doug too. It should have been monumental. This day should have brought the phone call of all phone calls from my oldest and dearest friend. None came. I spent my day trying to be very greatful.

Sometimes, given great disappointments, that is all we can do. We can also remember that even if that special person doesn't call, God doesn't forget these important occasions. People will let us down. It is inevitable. God will not. He never sleeps, never forgets, never fails. He never falls short of the goal. Beyond that, he longs for us to share everything with him. He can't wait to share every special moment with us. It should have been more important for me to share this day with God than it should have been for me to share it with Doug. Once again, I brought my burdens to God—last, not necessarily first. I asked his forgiveness and asked him to please fix what I could not. I never expected what would happen next.

February is always a big month here in Daytona. February in Daytona means Speed Week. We host a series of races including the "The Twenty-Four Hours Race" of Daytona and the infamous Daytona 500. It's a week long series of races that drives around 250,000 race fans to come to town. On the Sunday of the Daytona 500, Christ Community Church has a history of renting out a local ball park to have church in because our campus is located very near the speedway. Doug had called on Friday. His attorney of nearly three years had suddenly and without expectation, withdrawn from the case twenty days before trial. He needed me to come and help him try and talk the attorney into not quitting or alternatively to help find another one. We decided that I would come down on Sunday following Church. I did not want to miss church at the ballpark. It was important to my children.

Historically, it is always cold and rainy during Speed Week. This year was no exception. The kids and I were really looking forward to church at the ballpark though. It is exciting for them because there is a bar-b-que and games after.

Following the service, we ate dinner with some very old friends that picked that day of all days to visit our church. On the way home, the kids and I were talking in the truck. "Mom, can we get ice cream before you leave today?" my son asked.

I looked in the rearview to reply to him as he was sitting in the back seat. "Justin, you must be kidding me. It's freezing outside. Didn't you get enough cold at the ballpark?" The next thing that happened is a jumble of screeching, scraping metal, sounds of all kinds coming from every direciton. Coming through a major intersection, we were plowed into by another vehicle. I actually remember nothing about this accident. My little SUV was slammed from the passenger's side and then spun around on two wheels slamming into a four-foot city welcome sign. We landed so hard that three of the tires severed completely from the axels. The next few hours were a myriad of emergency medical people and tests. The kids were miraculously not harmed other than a few bruises. I had to be transported to the emergency room to be sure the shunt was not damaged. I also had no feeling in my legs.

After a few hours, I was released. The loss of feeling in my legs turned out to be shock and cold. It eventually returned. My SUV was completely undrivable. I did not have rental car coverage on my insurance. I was unable to successfully contact Doug to tell him about the accident. Doug lived two hours south of me and without a vehicle to drive the situation was now most certainly changed. Dad met me at home following my release from the emergency room. He asked about my intentions regarding the trip to Doug's. "Do you still plan on going to Doug's?"

"Well, I should. Maybe I'm not supposed to?" I replied, still in a slight state of shock.

"I know you. You will be miserable thinking that you're not helping him." Dad replied.

"You are probably right, but how will I get there?"

"I'll just have to drive you is all I know," my dad stated simplistically. I sat on the bed not really knowing what to do. After talking it over a little, Dad and I decided that he would drive me to Doug's, and I would worry about what to drive back after I got there. Doug had the added charm of being a licensed automobile dealer, and I was hoping he would have an extra car he was trying to sell that I might borrow while my car was being repaired or totalled. I was exhausted and sore when I arrived at Doug's house Sunday evening around nine o'clock. Doug was not home but his sister was. I said good-bye to my children and sent them along with my folks back to Daytona. Then I threw up and went to bed. I did not even wait for Doug to get home.

This started a series of daily vomiting episodes that would not stop for the next month. I could not eat or keep anything down. Apparently, the impact of the accident had caused some jarring of the tube which was just causing me constant discomfort and nausea. If I wasn't throwing up, I was doubled over in pain. The pressure of Doug's legal situation along with the pressure of our failing friendship did absolutely nothing to help me get past this physical challenge. On Monday, we met with the attorney. We showed up unannouced, but he was not at all surprised to see us there. We were unable to persuade him to stay with the case. This meant we had no choice but to find another attorney. There would be hearing on Wednesday of that week so that the Judge could hear arguments and decide whether or not Doug's attorney would be allowed to withdraw. I was under subpeona to appear before opposing counsel that same week. I drew up a motion requesting a continuation of thirty days for both Doug's case and my deposition in which time, Doug would try to retain new counsel. In the two or three days we had until the hearing, we began interviewing lawyers. This was a complex case and so each interview took several hours. We would get up very early in the morning, drive an hour and a half to two hours to get to the county where the lawsuit was filed, work all day and drive back late in the evening exhausted.

Doug was worried about my constant nausea and vomiting—genuinely worried. He was determined to find something I could keep down. South Florida is a wonderfully culturally diverse area, especially when it comes to food. Doug came up with the idea that I would be able to keep down something called seviche. Seviche is a peruvian dish of raw fish. Already I know it doesn't seem too appetizing, but he explained that the lemon juice it was cured in along with the very light spice choices of the dish would probably sit very well on my stomach. I could always trust Doug when it came to stuff like homeopathic treatments and food. Ususally the more bizzare things sounded, the more he was right. He found a peruvian restaurant near the attorney's office, and sure enough, I had a meal that not only could I keep down but that I thoroughly enjoyed. I could not stop expressing my thankfulness and noting how good the food was. Doug was laughing, and for the first time in a long while, there was some lightheartedness in our friendship.

I wound up staying the entire week. We had many conversations of great length. As the week ended, I needed to get back. Doug asked me, "What's the plan for getting you back to Daytona?" I told him rather simply "I don't really have one. I worried about how to get here. I was hoping you had an extra car you would be trying to sell that maybe I could borrow."

"I don't have any right now. Let me think a minute...I know, you can take my car."

"What will you drive Doug?" I asked.

"I'll drive Sarah's car," he answered. I was heading back to Daytona without having retained counsel which was very disturbing to me, but Doug and I were communicating much more effectively and we had found a reason to at least try and restore things. Doug wound up loaning me his personal vehicle to drive. He was working on a car for his daughter who would be turning sixteen in April and said that he would drive that one. I was both surprised and thankful. This was a big sacrifice for Doug. Doug was maticulous about his car. It was very comfortable, and I knew that Sarah's would not be. I was very appreciative. There was hope once again that our friendship might survive after all.

Over the next twenty-five days, I interviewed an additional eighteen attorneys, none of which worked out for this case. We were rapidly running out of time; Doug's case could not legally go forward without representation. He would have to give up after fighting for three years. In the meantime, I was juggling my new job and my health. Dr. Benezette was finally able to put me on a round of medication that caused the vomiting to subside. We still had to deal with stabbing pains, but at least I could eat.

Once again, God had taken me places I never would have gone on my own. If you could have seen my face the day of the accident and the look of stunned amazement at the state of my vehicle. All that kept going through my mind, was, *God...how much more? What else could I possibly endure? How am I going to function without a vehicle?* And I guess that is how the world would look at it. But as a Christian, you and I see things that the world doesn't see. First of all, Joyce happened to be taking the same route home so she was on the accident scene moments after it happened. She was with me in the emergency room. My dad lived down the street from the accident scene and was also there moments following the accident and was able to care for my children. Doug's attorney withdrawing from his case opened up a neutral avenue of conversation for Doug and I and forced us to work together setting aside differences in order to resolve a desperate situation. Furthermore, my destroyed SUV gave Doug an opportunity to give something back sacrificially. The sacrifical part touched my heart so much that I quickly began praying and asking God to restore this friendship and make it better than it was before and to allow me to sacrifice my anger at having been let down, even if Doug did not sacrifice his. Even the vomiting had significance. Doug now had a means of helping. He did what he was really good at by helping to resolve a medical condition. He was able to feel useful for the first time in a long while in my situation.

I had asked God to fix things. He replied, "I can do better than that!"

Time To Heal

I absolutely loved working for Don. I had over the course of my life had several management jobs including government work. I had not found anything that I enjoyed more than working for Don. Almost immediately, I brought on staff a long time colleague to head up the Information Technology Department. While that was my forte, I was finding it difficult to handle operations and IT so my friend Jeremy came to the rescue. Don was also always understanding (having walked through so much of my trial with me) of my medical limitations. He could look at me and tell if I was too tired to work or not feeling well, and he always put my health before my duties. I had gone back to work seven days after the last surgery and had never really taken the time any of my physicians would have recommended for healing. My life had been a whirlwind of circumstances. There had been no time for rest.

Jeremy suggested we call this book *Just Call Me Job.* While we have had lots of good laughs over that, I would not really characterize myself as one who had been chosen by God to represent him in a challenge against Satan. We live in a world that has been battered and scarred with sin. Every aspect of this earth is invaded with life-stealing sin. The events of my life are permitted by a sovereign God but are in part the result of living in a sin-infected environment. Germs caused the very beginning of my story. Germs became harmful after the introduction of sin into the Garden of Eden. The eco-structure of this earth was forever altered after the introduction of sin.

I was just pushing forward as much as I could as often as I could. My life was much better than it had been prior to the third surgery, but I was not overcoming some of the obstacles that seemed to me should have been overcome by this time. We had not overcome the stabbing pains the lower portion of the tube seemed to cause. We had made great progress on the nausea issue but had never completely resolved this issue.

I eventually made an appointment to go and see my gynecologist, Dr. Pamela Carbiener. She is a tremendous doctor, who is as insightful as she is caring. I needed to make sure that the stabbing pains were indeed the tube and not a device she had installed following my hysterectomy. She found that there was a large amount of bacteria present and immediately started me on a round of antibiotics. She also noted that the tube was creating a significant amount of scar tissue and suggested that before long that may become problematic.

In the meantime, I had upgraded my cell phone to one that was bluetooth adaptable. A day or so after using the bluetooth (which I found very convenient for a Type A personality like myself) I began to notice pressure building in my head. Being a Type A personality, I had the device on night and day. The pressure continued to build in my head. After a week or so, Jeremy asked me about the programmable aspects of the shunt. We reviewed them and then he quickly deduced that the bluetooth was interfering with the shunt. I spoke to Dr. Benezette about this possibility. He said, "It makes perfect sense. We need to obtain an x-ray to determine if the shunt opening has been effected." Dr. Benezette spoke with another neurosurgeon who was local to the Daytona Beach area about how to order the x-ray and what to look for.

Within a couple of days of the x-ray, I was making an emergency room run with my friend Belinda because the pressure had gotten so severe in my head. There was a new doctor in the ER whom I had never met. He was young, attentive, and very kind. We quickly brought him up to speed on my condition. He called Dr. Benezette to consult and then ordered pain medication and anti-inflammatory medication and nausea medication. Once they injectected the medicine into my IV, I started to cry. I had allowed the pain to go too long, and the medicine was an instant reminder of the state I had been in before the surgeries. Belinda held my hand and assured me it would be okay. Tears rolled down my cheeks. The ER doctor was concerned about what was causing the build-up of pressure and whether or not he should keep me for additional testing. Belinda and I were able to convince him that we were working on getting Shands to correct the problem by reprogramming the shunt and that we were confident of the cause. He agreed to let me go home but insisted that I come back immediately if things worsened. We assured him that I would. Belinda took me home. It took me two full days to get this medication out of my system. It had been so long since I had been given that dosage and combination of medicines that my system was no longer used to the heavy medication. These medicines just made me completely useless and kept me in an intoxicated type state.

Shands had been contacted, and at first was skeptical and did not want to give me an appointment. Dr. Benezette put in a second call at my request, and the next day I received a call from a familiar voice stating, "Dr. Wallace is no longer practicing at Shands. I will be assigning you to a new surgeon." I was to come up the following week, bring up the x-ray and be prepped to have it re-done at Shands. I agreed.

The following Tuesday, my daughter and I drove up to Shands. Justin stayed with my dad. We met the new surgeon who was a six foot three man of Chinese decent. He was very kind and asked me about what I thought the problem was. I was surprised after telling him that he was very open to my opinions. He suggested re-programming the shunt. I was stunned. I said, "Now?"

He said, "It works for me, you're here." He then told me that they had a new machine, which no longer required me to obtain an x-ray as follow up to confirm the shunt's opening. That was great news. The less exciting news was that he had never operated the machine himself. He proceeded to place the Star Trek like device on my head, which communicated instructions to the shunt on what setting to open the shunt to.

After five tries, he was successful at resetting the shunt. My head was sore from all the mashing on it, but this had been a relatively easy visit for me. The doctor warned me, "If our theory turns out to be incorrect, you will have to come back for all those nasty tests that you are so objectionable to." I nodded an affirmative understanding. This surgeon whom I already preferred over the last one then informed me, "Today is my last day at Shands." I told him of the difficulty for me in not having a surgeon and asked what I was to do if things did not go well after today? He said, "I will assign some follow up orders to have you placed with a department head surgeon."

I asked, "Why a department head?"

He replied, "Because the gentleman I am suggesting has been around forever and therefore you would likely have him for a longer period of time." This was good news as I was beginning to feel like I couldn't keep a surgeon to save my life.

After checking out, we proceeded to meet Selina for lunch. I had not seen her in some months now and hated to drive up that far and miss the opportunity. We had a lovely visit and then drove home. Within an hour of leaving Shands, I was already feeling relief from the pressure in my head. Driving home though, I was tired. Recovering from pain always brings with it fatigue. We don't realize how much effort our bodies put into tolerating pain. I had time to think of other trips home and what a difference this one was. I had time to worship with great music and to really thank God for his provision on this trip.

The following week, I would see Dr. Benezette, and the week after that I would see my gynecologist. Dr. Benezette was pleased with the shunt re-programming but was disappointed to hear we were losing the surgeon. I discussed with Dr. Benezette my visit with the gynecologist and her concern that all three physicians needed to be speaking with each other. Despite so much progress, I was still having stabbing pains from the bottom end of the shunt. Dr. Benezette started me on a medication called Topramax, which is an anti-seizure medication but could be used to sedate the nerve endings in the peritoneal cavity which he hoped would lessen the stabbings. The Topramax has some risky side effects that Dr. Benezette was careful to review with me. After a few days, the risky side effects began to appear, and Dr. Benezette's nurse gave me permission to stop the medication. We switched to another medication called Trileptal. In the meantime, I had my appointment with the gynecologist. The bacteria levels had dropped considerably, and she was pleased with the outcome of the re-programming as well. She did note, "There is even more scar-tissue that seemed to develop just since your last visit, and while the antibiotics seemed to have stopped this bacteria for now, I am concerned about future developments."

Also during this time, God had graced us at the eleventh hour with a new attorney for Doug's litigation. David Eltringham seemed to be diligent and had a very fresh perspective on this difficult case. That was not what I liked most about him though. I was most impressed with his powers of insight. He immediately told Doug, "This case has taken its toll on both of you, but mostly her. (David made this statement as he pointed directly at me.) I am immediately reducing her involvement in this case. She is no longer a witness. I'll inform Mr. Mattson." Michael Mattson was the lead attorney for the defendant in this case and the man seeking to depose me. This was of great relief to me at that particular moment. I also liked the way that this attorney astounded the opposing counsel.

This relief was good for my friendship with Doug as well. Perhaps with some distance between us, some of Doug's anger would subside. I had learned in recent weeks from some very wise people that at least part of Doug's anger was probably centered on the fact that his mother had died of brain cancer and that my circumstance was forcing him to relive something he never wanted to endure in the first place. Other than my children, I cannot think of any person on this earth that I care for more than Doug Williams. I would never want to be the cause of any source of contention for him. However, I confess that I have been more times than I care to remember. Knowing that I was a painful reminder of something very unpleasant for Doug made me sympathetic. It did not, however, make up for him not having been there when I needed him most. This comes down to a difference in thought processes between men and women. To my way of thinking, having been through something similar should have made him more sensitive to my situation and should have given him coping skills to help me. After long periods of time without improvement to my physical condition, Doug felt powerless to help. He had also been powerless to save his Mother. It occurs to me now that, to Doug's way of thinking, he was not a doctor and there would be nothing he could do to help me. Therefore, he would be better off staying home and praying for me when I had to go back to Shands for the second surgery.

I had started to notice that my prayers to God to change my heart were starting to have an effect. I had stopped trying to persuade Doug argumentatively to come around to my way of thinking. This allowed us to have more pleasant conversations. My not having to work night and day on his legal case freed up some of my energy so that I was not so tired. This allowed me to not be so frustrated with Doug. Doug and I have since that time gotten to spend some time together on several occasions all of which have been wonderfully pleasant. Our friendship had gotten some much-needed time to heal. I, however, had not gotten that same time.

After a few months time, Don let me know that my work with his company would be ending. This was no reflection on my work or on Don. Events had taken place, which would cause the company to close its doors. I took a deep breath and started praying about the next step. I don't have all the answers even today. I do know that God has never been caught off guard by my circumstances and he is not caught off guard now. I have watched as he has made so many things new in my life. Steven Curtis Chapman sings a song called "All Things New." This song reminded me often that God can make new that which we in our limited humanity cannot.[1] I have watched as God has worked to make things new in my life. He has made new and fresh my spiritual walk with him, my physical condition and my relationships with others. The next step for me will probably come in taking time to heal. My physicians have spoken to me about taking some time off to really recuperate. I think there is wisdom in those words. Ecclesiastes 3:1-3 (NIV) tells us that there is time for everything.

There is a time for everything, and a season for every activity under heaven: a time to be born and a time to die, a time to plant and a time to uproot, a time to kill and a time to heal, a time to tear down and a time to build.

It has been a long road, and although my efforts to be normal are commendable, it is wise to be realistic about my situation. Rest and healing are a part of God's plan. He intends for us to take that time. I am hoping that my time off will make me stronger than I have ever been and perhaps give me some fresh ideas about how to use my experiences to help others see God in their own situations. Everybody has situations and stories. God orchestrated these events so that I might be able to share them and help someone else who needs to know that he never does leave us or forsake us. He is with us always even unto the end of the age. I don't know where my story goes from here. It may be God's will for me to overcome this illness. I certainly hope that it is. If it is not God's will for me to overcome this illness, I hope my path, my efforts, and my life glorify him and lead others to trust him more. I hope in the preceding pages you have been able to see how he never left me and that you will know by this that he will never leave you either.

Lessons Learned
Along the Way

I've learned many things along the way. It only seems fitting that the last chapter of this book should share some those insights with you. *I've learned that one can go a very long time without going into Wal-Mart.* I think during one point of my illness, I went over six weeks without stepping one foot into that store. This is certainly no reflection on Wal-Mart. I happen to think that Wal-Mart is a fine institution. However, my point to making this one of the lessons that I've learned is that often we allow our lives to become so busy that our routines center around our weekly shopping trips. I used to joke in the checkout line at Wal-Mart that they should just payroll deduct my spending out of my weekly payroll to make things easier. I don't make that joke anymore. My priorities have been completely realigned, and my weekend time off does not center around the chores and shopping. Those things have their place but my time with my children is far more precious to me than anything else.

I've also learned that my relationship with God is far more important and significant than any circumstance in my life. If you have gotten yourself to a place of complacency about church attendance and fellowship with the saints, get yourself right and quickly. Realign your thinking! Find a new place to worship if necessary. God is a necessary part of your existence. Keep your faith and your relationship real and in the present. You don't know what circumstance you will find yourself in tomorrow. I've heard and repeated the old cliché that says all you have to do is die and pay taxes. That is not true, not really.

You have to live and live a life that glorifies God. One day you and I will stand before the Holy God and give an account of how we used our time and talents. I want more than anything to hear the words well done. I want my children to be there standing beside me. I want them to hear the words said to them. Life is really hard. I'll be the first to stand next to you and relate to this fact. Knowing that I am God's child gives the hardships purpose. I know that he does not waste a single hurt that we go through. Hold on to Jesus, He's holding on to you!

Witness right where you are. Your circumstance is an opportunity for you to be a witness. Be faithful with what you have been given, even if that which you have been given does not seem like a gift. Like the lady in the CT lab who caught me reading the book or the surgeon who operated on my son, you never know who is watching you and who you will be able to encourage through your circumstance. My children have watched me walk through this circumstance and more than anything my prayer is that God has been real to them in this. Who is watching you?

Giving should be sacrificial. You and I don't necessarily have the same gifts to give. Some people are blessed with monetary gifts. Others are blessed with musical talents. God tells us to bring the sacrifice of praise. Your gift may not be money or music. You most definitely have a gift to offer and your offer of the gift may require great sacrifice. The Pharisees gave a tithe of all that they had including the mint in their gardens. The widow only had two mites, and she gave it all. Which gift was the bigger to God? It is not the size of your gift by the world's measurement that counts. It *is* the size of your gift by God's measurement that is significant. Don't let the size of your gift prevent you from giving it. God sometimes places us on the receiving end of gifts. That is not always the most comfortable place for some of us. I am one of those people who is better at giving than receiving. I'm also terrible at asking. God has taught me through this experience that you do what you can but you ask for help when you need it. Failing to ask or failing to accept gifts offered may be denying someone who has a need to give. God may not have placed resources in your hands, but he has placed them in someone's hands. Take your pride out of the way and let God be glorified in the giving and the receiving.

Celebrate Birthdays and Special Occasions. They are important. Take every opportunity this life presents to celebrate every occasion possible. Include God in your celebrations. Make him the center of those celebrations. I did not celebrate my fortieth birthday well at all. I hated turning forty. I had just had the hysterectomy a few months earlier and felt completely unworthy in every way. Doug chose this occasion of all occasions to send me a bouquet of chocolates. Most women would be thrilled to receive such an unusual gift. I was devastated by them. First of all, Doug had over the years spoiled me with giant bouquets of Roses on special occasions. Now, turning forty, fearing all of the things (including weight gain) that all forty year old women fear, a bouquet of chocolates was the gift of fat hips. Poor Doug! I feel so bad for him now looking back on it. He got no joy out of that giving at all. Had I known what was ahead of me to come, I might have had a different viewpoint of both the gift and the birthday. Celebrate. Be Joyful. Be Thankful!

I've learned that God rarely tells us what's going to happen in the future. I've often thought that life would be easier if he did just tell us. Now I know better. Most of us would run the other way like a hurd of wild horses or like Jonah being told to go to Ninevah. Faith *is not* born out of knowing what is ahead of you. Faith *is* born out of knowing who it is that holds your future. Philippians 1:6 finds Paul declaring that "being confident of this very thing, that He who has begun a good work in you will complete it until the day of Jesus Christ." Faith is knowing who God is and who you are not. It is knowing that his work in you is good and for your good. I am confident that he is able to keep me until that day.

Release your expectations. On more than one occasion Pastor Matt had to remind me that I needed to give up my expectations. Don't put God in a box. Let go of what you want in exchange for what he wants to give you. That may sound easier than you think the act will be. I promise it is worth the exchange. God can do better than what you expect. Don't limit him to your human expectations. Your ways are not his. I would not have chosen my path, but I would not trade it now for the fellowship with God and his saints that has arisen from it. I also would not trade the reality of who he has become to my children through this experience. I'd endure this experience all over again for that reason alone.

Be real in your experience. God does not expect you to not feel, and he does not expect you to hide your feelings. Enduring your trial does not mean that you have be some sort of unaffected, stoic saint. Be real. Share your experience so that others can help you. Look for God's encouragement. He wants you to have it. He has specifically placed others in your path that will help to supply it.

Love others with a love that never ends. Mark Schultz sings a song titled "What Will You Do With The Time?" It begs the question, what will you do with the time that is left? It is a powerful song and hits straight to the heart. "Give the pain to Jesus and don't look back."[1] Give up the right to hurt others for hurting you. Jesus loves you with a love that never ends. It is a love that gave up everything to save you. Give up everything to save someone else. Don't give up through the tough times especially on those relationships that you know are worth everything. Love them as Jesus loved you, with a love that never ends. Extend forgiveness. It has been extended to you.

Know your limitations. Don't take on or keep what you cannot handle. Do your best with what you have but know what your limits are. I have a great friend—Karen Miller. One of my favorite things about Karen is that she always reminds me to know what my limitations are and to set my boundaries accordingly. This is great advice for almost every aspect of life. It doesn't mean that you don't shoot for your dreams or reach for the stars. It just means that you avoid stress as much as possible by not placing yourself in situations that you know exceed your limitations. It also means that if you have placed yourself in such a situation, you remove yourself as soon as possible. Be optimistic. Look at the bright side as much as possible, but realize your limits and ask for help beyond your limitations.

I've learned that there is great help in natural homeopathic treatments. I owe my life to my neurologist, Dr. Benezette. He is a great physician who truly cares for his patients. He is the first to be supportive of natural, homeopathic treatments. I don't think that the use of such has to exclude modern medicine. I think that both natural treatments and medicinal, pharmaceutical treatments can work together to bring the best relief. I believe (and this is strictly Annieology) that God has provided most if not all of what we need on this earth to heal ourselves. I believe that we have not relied on that or studied that concept nearly enough. We have relied so heavily on the pharmaceutical industry that we have abandoned our search for more natural cures in most cases. Natural, homeopathic remedies brought me great relief and were very soothing to me throughout this experience. I also found that some doctors are very open to the use of such. You should at least share these remedies with your doctor if you're considering using such options. Natural remedies in most cases can be much more cost effective that traditional pharmaceutical remedies (especially when insurance coverage does not apply).

It is completely true that these remedies themselves or at least to the extent of my knowledge at the time, were not enough to heal my condition completely. I needed a surgeon and a shunt. However, we made great success at beating the original staph infection with homeopathic remedies. Given time, we may find a natural cure for this illness.

I've learned that you never go wrong with encouragement. I shudder to think where I would have been without the encouragement I received along the way. I have heroes in Max Lucado, Mark Schultz, and Larry Burkette. I also treasure the personal one on one encouragement I received from my friends, my church family, and my dad. Making yourself available to encourage others will never be a wrong move. You may think your gift is small, but I promise as one who has received such gifts that none of them are small. They are each treasured. While I can never repay even the simplest kindnesses that were extended to me, I have asked God to bless each and every person who extended those kindnesses. The most difficult of relationships can be improved when we offer encouragement.

I've learned that there is nothing that God cannot do. The most important lesson I learned throughout this experience is how *big* God really is! There is nothing that He cannot do. He does not make mistakes and is never caught off guard. He loves me with an everlasting love. He works all things together for my good. I have all kinds of limitations. *My God does not.* He is bigger than my biggest strife. If I hold fast, one thing stronger than my strife is his grasp. I am his child and when I hurt, He loves me with the love of a parent. I hate it when my children hurt, but I hate it in a way that wants to take care of the hurt. God also wants to take care of our hurts. He wants us to be whole. He may not alter our circumstance in the way that we would like, but he will use our circumstance to his glory. He will make sense out of what seems senseless. He brings hope and peace to our situation. My prayer for you is that you will let him bring his hope and his peace to your situation.

Notes

Introduction:
1. Norman, Bebo, "Borrow Mine," *Try,* Brentwood Music, 2004.

Chapter 2:
1. Chapman, Steven Curtis, "Believe Me Now," *All Things New,* Sparrow Records, 2004.

Chapter 3:
1. Yancey, Dr. Philip, *Where is God When It Hurts,* Zondervan Publishing House, 1997.
2. Lucado, Max, *Facing Your Giants,* Thomas Nelson Publishing, 2006.
3. Schultz, Mark, "Back In His Arms," *A Night of Stories and Songs,* Word Entertainment, LLC, 2005
4. Schultz, Mark, "He's My Son," *Mark Schultz,* Word Entertainment, LLC, 2000.

Chapter 6:
1. Burkette, Larry with Michael E. Taylor, *Damaged But Not Broken,* Moody Press, 1996.
2. Crowns, Casting, "The Mountain of God," *Casting Crowns Duel Disc,* Tower Records, 2005

Chapter 9:
1. Schultz, Mark, *A Night of Stories and Songs DVD,* Word Entertainment, LLC, 2005.

Chapter 10

1. Chapman, Steven Curtis, "All Things New," *All Things New,* Sparrow Records, 2004.

Chapter 11

1. Schultz, Mark, "What Will You Do With The Time," *A Night of Stories and Songs,* Word Entertainment, LLC, 2005.